Also by John Rember
Traplines: Coming Home to Sawtooth Valley
Cheerleaders from Gomorrah: Tales from the Lycra Archipelago
Coyote in the Mountains

MFA in a Box

A *Why* to Write Book

John Rember

Dream of Things
Downers Grove Illinois USA

Published by Dream of Things
Downers Grove, Illinois USA
dreamofthings.com

Rember, John.
    MFA in a box : a why to write book / John Rember.
    p. cm.
    Includes bibliographical references and index.
    ISBN 9780982579428
1. Creative writing –Problems, exercises, etc. 2. English language –Rhetoric –Problems, exercises, etc. 3. Creative writing (Higher education). 4. English language –Rhetoric –Study and teaching (Higher). 5. Authorship. I. MFA in a box : a why to write book. II.Title.
PE1408 .R429 2010
808/.042—dc2222
2010929264

Dream of Things provides discounts to educators, book clubs, writers groups, and others. Contact customerservice@ dreamofthings.com or call 847-321-1390.

Cover design: Megan Kearney, Cartwheel Design Studio
Book design: Susan Veach

First Dream of Things Edition

For Julie,
who wears many hats in our marriage,
some of them gold.

Contents

Acknowledgments

I wish to thank the students of the MFA program at Pacific University Oregon for being the initial audience for these meditations. Their intelligence, wisdom, feedback, and friendship have shaped this book.

I am grateful to my friend and publisher Mike O'Mary for his encouragement and for his willingness to see this project through to completion. I couldn't and wouldn't have done it without him.

Finally, I owe a debt of gratitude to the generous teachers and colleagues who showed me how good and conscious and humane the life of a writer can be. I'm still trying to live up to their examples.

Introduction

MFA IN A BOX is not a How to Write Book. It's a *Why* to Write Book.

If you want a How to Write Book, two good ones are William Zinssner's *On Writing Well* and Richard Hugo's *The Triggering Town*. In my decades of teaching writing, I've consistently assigned those two books to my students. Another book I always assign is Diana Hacker's *A Writer's Reference*, because new writers make apostrophe mistakes. Editors view apostrophe mistakes the way they might view a worm dropping out of the nose of a corpse, and as far as they're concerned, the corpse belongs to the writer whose flawed manuscript they're reading.

This book is full of references to other writers and their works, and you may recognize the worm and the nose above as an allusion to *Gilgamesh*, one of the oldest stories in the world. It's a story about death and grief, and I consider death and grief so important to writers that I've devoted a chapter of this book to a meditation on *Gilgamesh* as a twenty-first century story.

If you read every work that I allude to in these pages, you'll have the foundation for a decent, if quirky, education in the humanities. You'll also be familiar with the struggles of brilliant minds to make meaning in a universe that can seem devoid of meaning. If you're struggling to make meaning out of your own experience, this book will help.

ALL OF THE CHAPTERS in this book had their origins in problems that either stopped my writing cold or that would have stopped it if I'd thought about them.

Here's an example: at one point in my teaching career I told my writing students, "You can't avoid nihilism, you have to go through it."

My glib words sounded good to me and may have sounded good to my students, but they wouldn't have sounded good to people who had studied Schopenhauer and Nietzsche, philosophers who had actually grappled with the problem. The old Schopenhauer joke goes that Socrates said the unexamined life is not worth living, and two thousand years later Schopenhauer discovered that the examined life isn't worth living either.

Actually, the phrase *Schopenhauer joke* is a joke.

So one of my chapters discusses what I meant by "going through nihilism," and the soul-destroying things that can happen to you if you try. As far as I know, none of my students actually did try to go through nihilism, which is a good thing.

These days, my less-than-glib caution to writers is that almost no one who dives into a belief in nothing makes it through to believing in something. Furthermore, if you write the truth about the world we live in, you're going to be facing more voids than just the blank screen in front of you. Now I tell my students, "Try not to write out of a totally naïve place. But don't write out of a place where you're so street smart that you don't believe in anything, because you'll quit writing or you'll kill yourself."

Too dark? Nothing in this book will be as dark as that place in the middle of a story where you're convinced that you're writing a bridge to nowhere, and that the idea of writing as an identity and occupation was a bad one in the first place.

Every writer faces that dark place, and a lot of them succumb to it. A good many people who invest years of their lives and tens of thousands of dollars in an MFA degree never write again, simply because they cannot follow a story into its own depths, or they fear that if they do, they'll never get back to daylight.

A big part of this Why to Write Book involves grappling with and defeating the terrors and discouragements that come when you have writing skills but can't project yourself or your work into the future. This book will give you solace in those dark nights of the soul, and it will give evidence that the sun eventually breaks the darkest horizon.

THIS BOOK tries to show and not tell. Whatever that means.

Somewhere far away and long ago, probably in the ancient city of Uruk, when Gilgamesh was its king, the first fiction workshop was held. When the workshop's first story was written on slabs of clay and passed around the group, fourteen of the fifteen people who read it inscribed the Uruk equivalent of Show Don't Tell in its margins.

If everyone agreed on the meaning of Show Don't Tell, there would be no reason for MFA programs. The great novels that people hold in their hearts would translate directly to the page, and then fly back off the page into the hearts of happy readers everywhere. That doesn't happen. One problem is that Show Don't Tell doesn't refer to what happens on the page. It refers to what happens in your reader's head when he or she looks at the page.

I don't claim that you'll know the ultimate meaning of Show Don't Tell by my last chapter, but you'll know more about what it means than you know now.

Parts of this book are a writer's memoir, parts of it are tales from my misspent youth, and parts of it are knowledge that I received from generous teachers. You will be relieved to know that I don't pretend that your path to writing will be the same as my path to writing.

Almost everything in this book will require that you translate it into your own terms. After all, I'm an old white guy writing in the middle of Idaho. Chances are that you're not one of those. So read with an eye toward changing my metaphors and images into equivalent metaphors and images from your own life. Above all, let my stories spark your own.

I HOPE that when you finish this book you'll be able to balance the deep despair of writing with the deeper joy of writing. I hope you'll find the courage to put truth into words. I hope you'll find reasons for being kind and intelligent in the presence of your readers and characters. I hope you'll understand that writing is a life-and-death endeavor, but nothing about a life-and-death endeavor keeps it from being laugh-out-loud funny.

I hope you'll finish this book with more reasons to write than not to write.

Finally, this book is in no way intended to replace a real MFA. If it were, I'd be charging a lot more for it. But if you have decided to become a serious and literary writer, it will give you glimpses of the terrain ahead, and an idea of the talent and will and good luck that you'll need to negotiate that terrain, and even some routes around the rough spots.

If you are an MFA student, this book will help you get more for your tuition money.

Regardless of who you are, it will give you reason to sit in that chair and to face the screen that has nothing on it. Yet.

John Rember
Sawtooth Valley, Idaho

1

Writing Violence

Reality is that which, when you stop believing in it, doesn't go away.
—Philip K. Dick

IT'S SIX HUNDRED MILES from my home in central Idaho to Forest Grove, Oregon. I've traveled those miles many times going to and from the June residencies of the Pacific University Low-Residency Master of Fine Arts in Writing program.

Six hundred miles means ten hours in the car, and you'd think that would be time enough to come up with the answers to every question about writing. But it doesn't work that way. Instead, you come up with more questions.

For example, as I've driven by the fences and concrete walls of the Oregon State Prison in Pendleton, I've wondered about the author and murderer Jack Henry Abbott, who wrote the prison memoir *In The Belly of the Beast*.

Abbott's memoir attracted the attention of the novelist Norman Mailer, who orchestrated a successful effort to have Abbott paroled in 1981.

Abbott's parole was less successful. Six weeks into it, he

stabbed a waiter to death for denying him access to a restroom. The stabbing prompted an ironic *mea culpa* from Norman Mailer, who said, in effect, that writers are shocked—shocked!—when the violence of their imaginations turns out to have a real world counterpart.

Abbott went back to prison for fifteen to life. It turned out to be life. He committed suicide in prison in 2002 after his second book didn't sell anywhere near as well as his first. He used a shoelace and a bedsheet to hang himself, which indicates determination, a certain amount of ingenuity, and an unwillingness to write a third book. He left a note, which may or may not have explored any of these things.

Norman Mailer was accused of romanticizing Jack Henry Abbott by portraying him as a talented artist caught up in the gears of an inhuman system.

In another side note to this story, Jack Henry Abbott's sanity wasn't questioned by the authorities until he killed himself. Then they called him crazy, indicating that suicide is the ultimate insanity defense.

A RELATIVELY BENIGN QUESTION that you ask when you drive through Pendleton at sixty-five miles per hour: how does someone like Jack Henry Abbott take the mindless violence of his life and make meaningful narrative out of it? A less benign question: what violence exists in the rest of us who are trying to write narrative, even if we've never been convicted of anything more serious than a parking violation? Less benign yet: how many stories are there behind the walls of the Pendleton prison, stories that will never get told because the people inside are so damaged that they cannot make meaning at all?

These questions imply that an ability to make meaning is good, the criminal mind of Jack Henry Abbott notwithstanding. When I juxtapose stories and meaning, I'm implying that stories are good, and that if we're not too damaged, we can form a narrative arc with a beginning, middle, and end, and we can tell it to other people, and their worlds will contain more meaning—if they're not too damaged to catch it.

But one more question, a question from the deep and the dark: what if most people, who aren't violent criminals, who live ordinary lives in a civilized culture, who pay their bills and go to their jobs and contribute to United Way—what if the mundane is a form of violence that has damaged these people so much that they can no longer tell stories?

If Jack Henry Abbott escaped nothing else, he escaped the mundane. And he was able to articulate the damage done to him over a lifetime of incarceration. In his letters to Norman Mailer, written at age thirty-seven, he noted that since the age of twelve, he had been free only nine and a half months. More than a decade of his imprisonment had been served in solitary confinement. But because his letters demonstrated that Abbott was sane and perceptive—that he could make sense after seeing and doing and having done to him what would render most of us mad—Mailer argued for his release.

Even after he had killed somebody for denying him the restroom, Abbott had his defenders. At the murder trial, where actor Susan Sarandon and writer Jerzy Kosinski appeared as character witnesses, Abbott told his victim's grieving widow that her "husband's life wasn't worth a dime." After Abbott's conviction, the widow said she was glad that he wouldn't be able to kill again.

Abbott's capacity for violence was his first defense against his world, but it wasn't his only defense. If you read *In the Belly of the Beast*, you understand that a culture that is supposed to protect human beings destroys some of them. Some people get caught in the gears, which is bad, but as they do they develop a sense of irony, which is good. Abbott wouldn't have become a writer without his sense of irony.

I don't think you can be sane without irony. I don't believe you can make meaning without irony. I don't think you can combat the violence of the mundane without irony. Without irony, your characters will be mute victims of circumstance, and over time, you'll be a mute victim of circumstance, too, not a writer at all.

Of course, in the long run, we're all mute victims of circumstance.

A PARTIAL LIST of the ironies attendant to the story of Jack Henry Abbott:

- In spite of the efforts of the prison authorities, Abbott did kill again.
- Susan Sarandon, who seems to be an otherwise benign person—somebody you'd like to hang out with, especially if you play baseball—named her son Jack Henry Robbins after Jack Henry Abbott.
- Jerzy Kosinski, whose novels contain a level of psychological and physical violence beyond the tolerance of a lot of readers, committed suicide in 1991 with barbiturates. His suicide note said he was putting himself to sleep for longer than usual. It was shorter and probably less articulate than the note Abbott left, which the prison

authorities still refuse to release. They're waiting for a call from their agent.

- Abbott's victim, a young man named Richard Adan, was an aspiring writer who had just had a play accepted for production.

- Norman Mailer knew more about non-fictional violence than he let on. He had stabbed his wife at a party in 1960, almost killing her. Mailer died in 2007, not a suicide, even though he had received the *Literary Review*'s Bad Sex in Fiction Award for his last book, *The Castle in the Forest*.

- Abbott's second book, *My Return*, expressed little remorse for any of his crimes and was used as justification to deny him parole at a 2001 hearing. So be careful what you put in your memoirs.

- Finally, if I'm correct to assume that telling stories is something that human beings will do if they're not too damaged, then there are lots of people out there way more damaged than Jack Henry Abbott, Jerzy Kosinski, and Norman Mailer.

SO YOU FIND YOURSELF on I-84 in Pendleton, Oregon, on your way to an MFA residency and you get caught up in the story of Jack Henry Abbott. You also gain some insight into the problem of staying in the Now if you're a writer. The Now is a prison in Pendleton where thousands of lives have been freeze-framed behind razor wire. The Now is the population of prisoner's spouses and children in Pendleton's cheap apartments. It's the abandoned buildings downtown and the recession-emptied campus of Blue Mountain Community College. It's the sputtering hum of your car in the 105-degree heat, the whine of its air-conditioner, the flashing lights of the Umatilla Tribe's Wildhorse Resort and Casino, and the steep grade of Cabbage Hill outside of town, where now and then a pickup driver with a trailer full of cattle won't downshift soon enough, and his brakes fail.

The Now is a violent place, and if you use pretty philosophical questions to insulate yourself from its violence, you're not going to see the Now at all. The Now will simply be a place you travel through while remembering the ironies surrounding a good writer who was a bad person and checking your memory once you get to a motel with Wi-Fi.

But before you start assuming that the Now is the fifteen minutes on either side of what your watch is telling you, consider this: if you are a writer, the most important characteristic of the Now is that it contains the past. Start telling a story and if you're not careful, you'll find yourself writing backstory. Start writing backstory and you'll find that you're not going back far enough. If you're a writer of *place*, you find the Now expanding to include the Pleistocene and beyond, because your characters seldom transcend the landscape. The Now is a tar pit at La Brea, and it's always giving up the perfectly preserved bones of what has fallen into it.

Jack Henry Abbott's isn't the only ghostly voice you hear on the trip from Sawtooth Valley to Forest Grove. Let's go back to central Idaho and start over, and see where we took a turn toward the dark, to get so ironic and so violent so soon.

WE LEAVE HOME in a June snowstorm. Snowstorms happen in Sawtooth Valley even when it's 105 in the desert west of Pendleton. Clouds fold over the Sawtooth Mountains, and streamers of snow come trailing down the canyons. Rocks roll down the road-cuts onto the highway, and deer and elk begin to move through the mists.

I drive slowly during June snowstorms, because sometimes people in giant SUVs will move into your lane to avoid rocks or cow elk or fawns, even when they see you coming.

Thirty-five miles from Stanley, where the road meets the South Fork of the Payette, the river that comes out of the north end of the Sawtooths, the past becomes the present. I am hit with a memory from the summer of 1965: my family is constructing new trail along the headwaters of that river, in a remote part of the Sawtooth Wilderness, twenty-four miles from the nearest road.

I'm fourteen. I'm living in a tent and most days I'm looking at the ass end of a harnessed workhorse, guiding a one-sided plow, peeling virgin hillside out and down to make a path for hikers and horsemen. And yet I'm not far from civilization. B-52 bombers fly over, dropping glittering chaff that makes spindrifts in the sunlight and hangs in the trees like tinsel.

That's forty-five years ago, is what I'm thinking as I wake from memory, twenty miles later. We're near the town of Lowman, once a mining and timber town, now a retirement community.

Not everything has changed. Some of the B-52s that dropped aluminum chaff on us are still flying. But some of their original pilots have died of old age. I've gotten a bit older myself.

In Lowman, we drive by fenced-off mounds decorated with radioactive warning signs. Underneath them lie great piles of uranium tailings. Before the topsoil was brought in and the fences were put up, people in Lowman used the tailings for backfill around their foundations and as surfacing for their driveways, and I remind myself to invest in a Geiger counter if I ever decide to buy a house in Lowman.

Downriver, after fifteen miles of whitewater, we pass a dam site that the Army Corps of Engineers evaluated during the 1950s, when they examined every stream in the country for hydroelectric potential. Their excavations are visible on the other side of the river, tunnels just a few feet above the water, where they drilled deep into the rock to see if it would anchor a dam five hundred feet high and a quarter mile wide in case oil ever stopped flowing from the Middle East.

When we get to Boise we stop at Costco. In that giant warehouse, with its racks of goods stacked to the ceiling, I fall into another memory: I'm surrounded by piles of Civil Defense supplies stored in the Sun Valley bus garage during the winter of 1962. My father drives one of the Sun Valley ski buses, and some days I wait in the garage for him after school. Fifty-gallon drums of crackers and water are stacked against the outside walls. The water is supposed to be a shield against radioactive fallout. The crackers are supposed to be equally effective against postwar starvation.

I still find it comforting to go to Costco and buy a year's supply of anything.

But we've got an MFA residency to go to, so we limit our purchases to wine and gasoline and get back on Interstate 84, one of the segments of the Eisenhower National Defense Highway System. As Allied commander during World War II,

Eisenhower was impressed by how the Germans used their autobahns to move military supplies and personnel, and he wanted something similar for his own country.

Our autobahns are designed to allow for the quick evacuation of American cities prior to the detonation of nuclear bombs in their centers. Throughout the entire system, one mile in five is straight, so that it can be used as a continent-wide airstrip in times of war. The section we travel is much straighter than that, at least until we get to the Columbia Gorge.

But before that, we pass 40 miles south of the 586-square-mile Department of Energy Hanford Reservation, where 56 million gallons of radioactive waste are stored in 177 underground tanks, some of them leaking. It's also a storage area for at least 4.6 million pounds of spent nuclear fuel, material that has to be stored in deep pools to keep it from melting into a critical mass, burning down to ground water, and drifting over the Northwest as radioactive steam and smoke.

It's also the location of 120 square miles of contaminated aquifer, the result of 440 billion gallons of liquid radioactive waste pumped directly into Hanford wells. Twenty-five tons of plutonium are there, much of it lost in the pipes and waste pits of Hanford's industrial maze. It's in the soil, plants, and the river. Plutonium-laden silt will pour over the Columbia's Celilo Falls if the McNary, John Day, and The Dalles dams are ever breached and fast-running waters cut down through the layers of reservoir mud.

Hanford isn't visible from I-84, but a few miles later, we can see the bunkers of the Umatilla Chemical Depot, which contain a collection of poison gasses and their delivery systems of rockets, artillery shells, and aerial sprayers. From the autobahn, we can see the earth-covered bunkers that contain all these things. There are a great many of them, lumps in the landscape stretching to the horizon. Inside them, enough poisons to kill all the mammals on the planet. They represent only 12 percent of the U.S. chemical-weapons stockpile and are due to be destroyed by incineration at a date that recedes into the future.

As we drive farther toward the ocean, I become aware of other, less obvious artifacts of war. Certainly the cities of Richland, Kennewick, and Pasco wouldn't exist without Hanford, and without the defense spending brought into Oregon by its congressional delegation, Portland would be a far smaller and less vital city.

We get tangled in traffic in Portland. I'm glad there isn't a nuclear evacuation going on, because it would make the traffic even worse.

Approaching Forest Grove, I conclude that if I'm going to write about the Now, I'm going to have to place my characters in a world that is a Cold War artifact. I'm going to have to consider that my characters are products of violence, even if they didn't spend their grade-school years ducking and covering under their desks or deciding which of their classmates they would go home with if their parents had been killed in a nuclear war. That shock of recognition that I experience when faced with the iconic skull scenes of the *Terminator* movies suggests that I rest on a substrate just as violent and criminal as the one on which the late Jack Henry Abbott rests.

IT'S DISTURBING to think that your world rests on violence. When I advise new writers, I encounter people who find it difficult to resolve the conflict in their stories. Nothing much happens in many of the stories I read. If the conflict has to be resolved by violence, the writer often as not leaves the scene. No one is there to guide the good guys into contact with the bad guys, and they instinctively avoid each other. Sometimes the bad guys are on vacation. Sometimes they're good guys in disguise. The last page of many stories I see is a lot like all the other pages: scenes happen, characters engage in dialogue, but nobody's life—least of all the writer's—is transformed.

The bad guys, if they show up, are cartoonlike and easily defeated. They don't hurt anybody. Nobody loses anything they can't ever get back. Magical realism is used to make the world a safer place for children, which even the children find boring and untrue and lacking in wonder.

It's as though the writer is a big unsmiling cop waving motorists around a particularly bloody accident on the Interstate: "Nothing to see here, folks. Keep moving."

When a writer puts a lid on the Now and says that the universe will continue with business-as-usual, stories die.

And when stories die, writers die. Camus called it philosophical death, by which he meant that when you deliberately set aside your sense of irony and cease to struggle against the absurdity of having a god's mind in an animal's body, the animal wins. You become flesh animated by nothing but tropism. What gives our god's mind sustenance is our willingness to be Prometheus in the face of Zeus. We disobey, we rebel, we ignore pleasure and seek out pain, we give fire to people who use it to upset the order of the universe and we go to our inevitable punishment only regretting that we got caught.

Writers are the cops who, instead of waving us on when we pass the accident, strip off their uniforms and jump up and down in black vinyl lingerie and say, "Stop your car. You gotta see this. Arms and legs are lying all over the blacktop, and we found a head in a motorcycle helmet stuck in the crotch of a tree. I've never seen so much blood. Look at this shit! Holy Cow!"

You don't have to write about violence all the time. But you do have to write about the world, and the world is a conflicted place, and often enough those conflicts are resolved by violence. You have to adopt an imperative of consciousness, which at its most basic means you pull the lid off the truth rather than sit on it.

Woody Allen says half of life is just showing up. For a writer, the other half is paying attention. The writer's most important function is bearing witness to what is real—to what hasn't gone away, even though you've stopped believing in it.

For example, if your readers drive by the miles of earth-covered bunkers of the Umatilla Chemical Depot, they need to know that those bunkers are not potato cellars. Nor was the Umatilla Tribe building funeral mounds about the time Lewis and Clark passed through. Giant plutonium-mutated prairie dogs have not escaped from nearby Hanford. What they are is evidence that two great and inhuman bureaucracies—one Soviet and one Capitalist—built millions of chemical weapons and biological weapons and nuclear weapons over fifty years of the twentieth century, and by the end of that time they had become twins, even down to the details of their collapse.

You don't have to write about collapsing civilizations if you're a writer, but it might be wise to lay in a carton of pencils and a stack of legal pads in case your computer uses electricity.

Consciousness asks that we consider the damage that our collective past has done to our individual present. If you're a writer placing your characters in the Now, you should know that the Now contains corroding stockpiles of weapons that won't get into the wrong hands as long as two corrupt and decaying economies continue to function.

LET'S LOOK at two connections between a capacity for violence and literary gifts.

The first connection comes out of structural theory, and it's been explored by Roland Barthes in a work called *Camera Lucida* and by Susan Sontag in *On Photography*, and it concerns the reduction of a three dimensional world to two-dimensional light and shadow, and what that reduction does to viewer and viewed. Sontag says photography turns its viewers into voyeurs, and its subjects into whatever it is voyeurs look at.

Barthes takes photography further toward the rendering of the world and the people in it. He is interested in photographs that contain the seeds of their own destruction, usually an image that violates the larger background of the photo itself. A bit of a photograph will betray its whole, exposing the whole endeavor as a flattened fraud.

Fraud or not, Barthes implies photography can turn the world into an ersatz version of itself. Painting becomes manipulated photorealism. Sculpture becomes a photographic object. Writing becomes camera work. Plays become screenplays. Our lives become ghostly light and shadow on flat film, and we cannot tell if we're in the photo or looking at it.

As a ski patrolman at Sun Valley I would pick up injured

people on the slopes, put them in a toboggan, slide them at high speed down to a waiting ambulance at the base lodge, and then ride with them in the ambulance to the hospital. Until they were lifted on a gurney and wheeled into the emergency room, they would be quiet and attentive and able to stand their pain. But once in the emergency room, all hell would break loose. They were finally in a situation that they had seen on TV, and they knew how to act. The histrionics began.

My injured toboggan passengers finally had a frame and a focus and a self image for their experience, one supplied by hospital soap operas. They no longer had to pay attention to what was happening to them—they could take it from there on memory alone. But they had less of self and more of image in the ER than they had had in the toboggan.

Once photography was invented it became difficult for writers not to use its conventions. Writers capture their characters. Writers frame scenes. Writers visualize narrative characters as cameras, and writers become adept at looking at the world through authorial lenses and filters. In my description of the journey between central Idaho and coastal Oregon, I'm using a filter that allows me to see the world as an artifact of the Cold War. That filter is a technical device. It's also a violation of creation itself, and it's probably a violation of the delighted child I once was, the child who first saw the world as green, whole, and nurturing.

God knows what violence Jack Henry Abbott had to do to his nine-year-old self just to get the first paragraph of his autobiography to the page.

Why do readers put up with this sort of thing? All this confusion between subject and object means that, at least for the moment of reading, readers are coerced into viewing their own lives through a viewfinder. Their world is framed, cropped, altered, distorted, and often enough betrayed by the writer.

If you're the writer doing the coercing, it helps if you look at readers as you might look at sophisticated collectors of photography. Readers are aware of your flattening, your cropping, your betrayals of the world. They search out your deliberate distortions in the illusion you create, and examine your use of technical devices to accomplish your ends. Your readers call what results your *vision*.

In this way of looking at things, technical skills aren't just part of what a writer has. They are *all* a writer has. To the extent your skills shape your perception of the world, you need to get used to your work being a form of violence.

A second connection between violence and literary gifts is more practical. It has to do with getting up in the mornings and not being paralyzed by thoughts of nerve gas, CIA torture memos, or chemical weapons that the Russian mafia may or may not have sold to Al Qaeda, or nuclear weapons in North Korean fishing boats off the coast of Oregon.

Jack Henry Abbott and Norman Mailer and Jerzy Kosinski aside, writers like Cormac McCarthy and Flannery O'Connor and Joyce Carol Oates and Raymond Carver are able to function even when they're writing about the mundane and facing the violence that lies under it. Much of their violence starts out of ordinary situations—look at Carver's "What We Talk About When We Talk About Love" as a good example of what can happen when friends get together for a little gin and reminiscence. They end up doing open-heart surgery without anesthesia.

O'Connor's "A Good Man Is Hard to Find" ends with a family on a road trip being murdered by a psychopath, and her gentle readers cheer when the grandmother gets it. McCarthy's *The Road* is a travelogue through savagery. Oates dedicates her story of a young girl's destruction, "Where Are You Going, Where Have You Been," to Bob Dylan—in lieu, I suppose, of dedicating it to the women who refused to see the violence against women in Dylan's poetry. There's a fair amount of misogyny in Joyce Carol Oates, and that's likely why she could see it in Bob Dylan.

What makes these writers functional is that when their stories lead them to violence, they embrace it. I don't imagine that Flannery O'Connor liked being conscious of her own murderous rage at her world and at the people who tried to be normal in it, but there it is, in black and white, in story after story. Maybe Cormac McCarthy likes writing about post-nuclear cannibalism, but his work seems less sadistic and more informative when I consider it from within the boundaries of the Umatilla Chemical Depot.

Every successful writer has the *courage* to confront the violence of the mundane.

Courage is the right word here. A page into writing a story, it's possible to think you'll never be able to face the violent implications of what you've put down. So you write a new first page. But it's better to stick with that first version and the ending it contains. Do it, and you'll rise from the blood and gore of a final draft and realize it's just a story. It can't hurt you anymore.

Successful writers know the difference between artifact and the world that spawns artifact. They can still glimpse the shadow of God's earth beneath the suburbs, and the flowing river beneath the reservoirs, and the tribal footpaths beneath the blacktop, even while they're writing about suburbs and reservoirs and blacktop.

That's why you should avoid the real temptation, once you learn how to write scenes and dialogue, to let them become your reality. It's a step on the way to becoming a writer, but it isn't the final step. The final step is when you realize that writing is all artifice, and when you're good enough at artifice, you can pay attention to what lies beneath it.

One of the reasons I like the effect photography has had on writing is that it makes artifice explicit, and turns writers into artisans with an illusion to create.

Rules for Writers

Jack Henry Abbott's Ten Tips for Writing in a World That Won't Give You the Key to the Restroom

1. Know that what you put on the page isn't reality. What you put on the page is an artifact you hope your reader will accept as real for a while. But the story ends. The book is put down, and only your reader is able to say whether it was worth the time to read it.

2. Embrace the conventions of photography. Use frames, focus, lenses, shutter speeds, slow-motion, camera angles, strobe-lights, studio backdrops, negative space, and Photoshop. Take the time to compose images. Remember that some images are more interesting than others. A series of still shots can be put together in sequence to form narrative.

3. If a part of your story doesn't puncture or betray another part, you haven't finished the story.

4. What you think the world is or want the world to be can overwhelm your perceptions of the Now. Don't let it. Your perceptions are all you have that are truly your own. One crystal-clear vision is worth more to your reader than a dozen brilliant conclusions. Let your reader draw the brilliant conclusions from your vision. You'll both be happier.

5. It's okay to have a savage sense of irony. A sense of irony is an awareness of the difference between the way things are and the way things are supposed to be. The bigger the difference, the more savage the irony.

6. Don't let your reader have a more developed sense of irony than you do. Other ways to put this: don't take anything for granted that your reader doesn't take for granted. Don't be soppy stern about something your reader finds funny.

7. Don't be afraid to be a criminal at the keyboard. You wouldn't want to write if you didn't have criminal tendencies. Writing is rebellion, a defiance of the order of the universe. If Zeus's punishment for your defiance seems not to fit the crime, just remember that your liver will be as good as new tomorrow.

8. Much rewriting and editing is simply improving the signal-to-noise ratio of a story until a reader can stand to listen. Static comes in many forms, among them vagueness, wordiness, avoiding conflict, dialogue that doesn't carry the story, and self-indulgent authorial intrusion. You can never get rid of it completely, but over a number of drafts you can give your reader an idea of what distinct thing you are witnessing.

9. Read people whose ability to perceive hasn't been undermined by cultural Photoshop, who understand the violence of the mundane. Four books that help to perceive the violence of everyday life are:
    - R.D. Laing's *The Politics of Experience*
    - Albert Camus's *The Myth of Sisyphus*
    - Ernest Becker's *The Denial of Death*
    - Peter Hoeg's *Borderliners*

    These books will help you with your Promethean Rebellion.

10. Remember that for 250,000 years of human history, unruly
    children were tossed out of the cave to play with the bears
    and wolves and lions. Writing will run into taboos that are
    deep in your genes. When two of your characters are about
    to say things to each other that will destroy their friendships
    and marriages and lives, you'll feel like you're about to be
    tossed out of the cave. But your readers will be just as scared.
    They'll be paying serious attention to the story you're telling.
    That's a good thing. That's the best part of telling a story.

2

The Writer as Outsider

"God!" he thought, "What a job I've chosen."

—Franz Kafka

HERE'S MY EDITED VERSION of Hans Christian Andersen's *The Little Match Girl*. With apologies to Raymond Carver, it's now called *What We Talk About When We Talk About Matches:*

> A cold, snowy, dark New Year's Eve. A small girl with no hat or shoes carries unsold matches down a city street.
>
> Snow covers her hair and freezes her feet. She looks in bright windows and smells roast goose.
>
> She sits against a cold stone wall. If she were to go home without money, her father would beat her.
>
> With numb hands, she lights one match. She sees and feels a great warm parlor stove. The match goes out and the stove disappears.
>
> Another match: she sees a table laden with a stuffed roast goose. The goose jumps off the table and walks toward her, a knife and fork sticking out of its breast. The match goes out and the goose disappears.

Next match: a Christmas tree with candles in its branches. The match goes out and the Christmas tree disappears, but the candles remain as stars. One of them falls and leaves a bright tail across the sky.

"Someone is dying," the girl thinks, and remembers her dead grandmother, who once told her shooting stars marked deaths.

Next match: her grandmother appears, alive, beautiful, and loving. The girl lights more matches. Her grandmother embraces her and carries her to God, where cold and hunger and fear don't exist.

New Year's Day: passersby find a small frozen smiling corpse, surrounded by burnt matches.

Raymond Carver's editor would be proud. The story has gone to 223 words, from a thousand or so.

HERE'S WHAT Hans Christian Andersen feels at this moment: his carefully crafted story, so full of imagination and detail and meaning, has been reduced to a skeleton. He's dismayed. He's angry. So much of what he put into the story has been taken out. He calls out to the nearest angel (because he's in heaven now): "How the hell did an editor get up here?"

If you have worked with an editor, you understand how he feels. Often enough, a rich, full story comes back shorter and full of holes, with its beginning gone and its ending paragraph chopped to a single line, a line that you didn't think was important. Now your editor is saying it's the most important line of the story. Now you have holes to fill. Now you have darlings to mourn.

Your story has been subjected to something violent and

reductive, and it's hard not to feel that you've been subjected to something violent and reductive, too. Worse, you are confronted with evidence that your editor is seeing something in your story that you didn't see when you wrote it. Enter all the changes, delete all the things that have been crossed out, print out a hard copy and see what it looks like, and sometimes you'll discover, to your embarrassment, another story that lies within your story— the real story—but that doesn't feel so good either, because you couldn't see it until it was pointed out for you.

WHEN I BEGAN thinking about writers being little match girls, I was coming off a long winter. My home is 6,500 feet above sea level, and on the first of May there was still a four-foot drift in our front yard. We heat with wood, and over the winter we made many trips to the wood pile, sometimes in the middle of blizzards, sometimes in the middle of cold, clear mornings when our wireless thermometer had flatlined because it only goes down to minus 21 degrees Fahrenheit.

So, on one of those flatlined mornings, I was sitting at the computer in my bathrobe when I noticed the room was getting cold, and not just because I had been editing out all the warm and happy parts of a student's story. A cloud had just blocked the morning sun. The fire had burned down to embers. The wood-box was empty. I looked for my slippers but couldn't find them. I decided that I could run to the woodpile with bare feet, grab an armload of wood and be back inside before frostbite set in.

I ran out, gathered a big enough armload that I couldn't see over it, and ran back to the door. I managed to hold onto the wood and grab the doorknob. Locked.

So I bumped the wood against the door, careful not to break the glass, hoping that my wife, Julie, would hear. She was working at her computer, in her office, with the door closed. She didn't appear.

I banged the load of wood on the doorframe, and after a minute or so, she showed up, looking at me in my bathrobe and bare feet.

"Sorry," she said, "We don't need any matches. Go away."

THE LITTLE MATCH GIRL JOKE is a part of our marriage. Sometimes I'm the little match girl, sometimes Julie is, but whenever the little match girl appears we're reminding ourselves that Julie and I each have the power to exile the other to a place that is cold and full of hunger and fear, and we choose not to do it. It's one of those things that makes us deeply grateful for each other's kindness, and it makes each of us want to nurture our own kindness toward the other.

THE SNOW was still on the ground when I sent an email to a colleague, catching him up on what had gone on during the semester. I had sent two manuscripts to my editor, but hadn't heard a word. It had been three months—but who was counting?

I told my colleague that I had gotten through the instant-return danger period, and the pass-it-around-the-office hopeful period. I was now into the he-hasn't-even-read-it despair period, and working on the he'll-be-sorry-when-I'm-famous-in-two-hundred-years revenge period.

My colleague wrote back to say he understood that sequence all too well, and I believed him. I believed him because even if you win the Pulitzer or the Booker prize, some editor can sit on your manuscript for six months and then send you an email that says, in effect, "That last book of yours we published? That was your last book."

At that point the writer stands in the position of the little match girl, hatless and shoeless and looking through a window at a publishing party, where the fire is glowing in the stove, the table is laden with steaming cider and hot spiced wine and goose and fruit, and there's music playing and people are looking into each other's eyes and it's the beginning of love—between your editor and some other writer, some writer that you vaguely remember being mean to back in a writing workshop, years ago.

But you're the one standing out in the cold, and nobody is running to let you in, because the operative principle isn't love in this world, it's finance, and all you have of value is your little collection of pages that nobody wanted. So, to keep warm, you take a page out of your threadbare coat and set it on fire and hope you see, in its flames, a better world than the one you're in. When it burns to ashes, you light another. People look out of the window, see what you're doing, and avert their eyes, because you're ruining the party.

I DISTRUST METAPHORS—and not just because some of them lead to unbridled self-pity. It's because metaphors tend to take stories and, in a reductive process, turn them into neat packages. In this case, it's the writer's whole identity that gets reduced to heartbreak. When that happens, it can become terribly hard to write, hard enough to make you quit writing and go to work in a meat packing plant or something. That may be more of a warning to avoid self-pity than to avoid metaphor, but if self-pity gets combined with metaphor, it's a lethal combination and you should stay away from it.

That's not to say that something can't be learned from seeing writers as little match girls. As much as we writers pride ourselves on our cultural antennae, our sixth sense for nuance, and our ability to act as a sensitive flame when a new character walks into one of our stories, it is our *out*sight—the vision of the outsider—that allows us to know all the details of the loving gaze, the soft-spoken endearment, the vintage of the wine on the counter, and the variety of cheeses in the hors d'oeuvres weighing down the table. If you're sitting outside the glass, starving and freezing your ass off and thinking that everyone who ever loved you is dead, you *see* better, however briefly. People on the inside are having too good a time to pay attention.

There is a school of artistic criticism that says that reality is better apprehended from the margins. Outsider art—art constructed by autistic or schizophrenic or brain-damaged people who are unable to apprehend the context that their art is viewed in—has been in vogue for a couple of decades now. It trades on the idea that poor little match girls have a vision that the spoiled daughters of rich merchants can never have.

Not too far down this road is the idea that poverty, loneliness, alienation, and victimhood can be a good thing if you're a writer.

Some critics have taken this idea to an extreme, and suggested that alienated misfits create purity in solitude. They're immune to the competitive worries of the rest of us, and the pathetic desire for fame, and the ugly pedestrian hunger for money. So if you combine your writing with a normal life, one with decent relationships with other people, a job with benefits, and a house that keeps the rain off and the cold out, your art won't be as good as if you worked in painful solitude, leaving empathy, love, and affection to people not so dedicated to creation.

These critics have a point. In my home state of Idaho the deaf, mute, and probably autistic artist James Castle produced drawings of astonishing complexity and beauty and power using spit, ashes, and chewed up colored paper. His works are often on tattered envelopes he salvaged from post office wastebaskets. But they are masterpieces of perspective and light, doorways into entire universes.

The works of James Castle make me realize that each human being, no matter how damaged, is a universe. But Castle found a way to let us into the universe he contains without having to turn to us and become aware of our awareness of him.

ARTISTS LIKE CASTLE represent a frightening option for writers, because he does what we would like to do, which is to remain focused inward, transfixed by the beauty of our own perceptions.

But it's important that we remain able to turn our eyes away from the inner landscape, no matter how hypnotizing the brilliance of our own visions. We need to see the people we are writing for as clearly as we see our inner landscape. So if we have to stand outside of comfortable and happy insiders, we also have to stand outside of outsiders as well. We have to achieve the consciousness of the story and not just the author.

Two literary and social critics relevant to this discussion are

Antonio Gramsci and Mikhail Bakhtin, who talk about how a marginalized consciousness can disturb and dislocate the people at the center of power. The key word is consciousness. It doesn't do you any good to be marginalized if you're not conscious. Gramsci talks about the anesthesia of the normal, or what I call the imposed sensory deprivation of consensus reality. Bakhtin talks about the rich carnival of voices that will come from the despised, the grotesque, and the misshapen, if only we allow them to speak.

One caution about reading literary critics: the consciousness of the artist is not the consciousness of the critic. You can read Gramsci and Bakhtin, who are brilliant writers focused on rich literary traditions, but after you've read them you won't write like Boccaccio or Dostoevsky. You'll write like Gramsci and Bakhtin. If you want to write like Boccaccio—and I hope you do—read Boccaccio. If you want to write like Dostoevsky, read Dostoevsky.

A COUPLE of stories here, one encouraging and one horrific:

One summer when I was working in Sun Valley, Idaho, the Yale Repertory Theatre came to town for six weeks of workshops and performances, sponsored by the Sun Valley Center for The Arts and Humanities. The playwright Jack Gelber came with them, and he put on a workshop for members of the community. I was accepted into the workshop, and we spent five of those six weeks writing plays. During the sixth week the actors of the Yale Repertory Theatre did cold readings of our work.

Gelber was a good teacher. I learned about the importance of structure that summer. If a play isn't structured right, it will have flat spots in it and your audience will go to sleep or leave.

Conflict isn't what builds in a play, because conflict should be there from the beginning. It's *intensity* that builds from scene to scene and act to act. A line of dialogue needs to be obliquely related to the line of dialogue that went before it—the more oblique the better, as long as your audience still gets the relationship. Also, reversals of plot are comic devices that will let you get to tragedy you couldn't get to otherwise.

What I learned in the sixth week was that good actors could take my halting, half-formed, almost mute characters to the stage and turn them into living, breathing, and sensitive human beings. I hadn't realized that I was such a good writer until I saw what the members of the Yale Repertory Theatre could do with my work. I became a sort of reverse Prufrock: "That is what I really meant, after all."

I learned that being a writer doesn't mean you have to do it all. There are people who can help you. Later on I learned that actors are just readers on a stage. And when the readers take the stage, in a comic reversal that allows you to approach a level of meaning you couldn't get close to otherwise, the writer becomes a member of the audience.

Here's the story: at the end of the workshop the writers and the actors got together for a party. The play I wrote had been performed the afternoon before, and my narrative character was a fat boy in a fraternity, admitted into the fraternity because he was the only guy on campus who could have real conversations with women. His fraternity brothers accepted him because he could get them dates. Some of them brought him along on dates so the women would have someone to talk to. Of course, at some point, the fat boy would get kicked out of the threesome and the other two would have sex. My play was a sort of a grotesque one-act version of *The Sun Also Rises.*

(Which brings up some painfully-arrived-at advice I have given to writing students: Adult Situation, Adult Sensibility, Adult Sexuality, Adult Voice. Don't write about fraternity boys. Don't write about children in the bodies of adults. For that matter, don't let those children spend all their time drinking in Spain and Paris if you can help it. Do look at Hemingway's dialogue, because Hemingway's dialogue is the beautiful baby in his bathwater.)

Back to the end-of-workshop party: the conversation got around to what it feels like to be the fat boy in the fraternity, the one who sees and knows things but can't act on his desires, in the middle of a bunch of people who can act on their desires but don't see things and don't know things.

And the members of the Yale Repertory Theatre—the talented and beautiful people who had made my poor play come alive—started telling stories of being rejected in junior high school and high school and college, of not being cast in plays because the director was sleeping with whomever did get cast, of parents who loved brothers or sisters best, of being blackballed by sororities, of not being allowed to play at a friend's house because the friend's parents looked down on your parents, of being bullied in the sandbox, of not being among the ones allowed to play horsie in kindergarten when everyone else was playing horsie—there were far more of these stories, and it was as though they had all happened that afternoon, if you were to go by the exquisite detail of their memories and the anger and pain that came with them. Today when I look at an actor giving a brilliant performance I wonder if I'm not also looking at a person who has a little match girl in him, and she's burning her last match.

THAT'S the encouraging story.

The other one—which I will try to tell from an adult's sensibility—is from when I was a socially inept junior in high school, in Hailey, Idaho, in 1966. The school had a tradition of holding a Sadie Hawkins dance every October, a dance where everyone would dress up as characters from Al Capp's *Dogpatch* cartoon strip.

Dressing as a *Dogpatch* character was a matter of going back through the clothes you refused to wear to school anymore, sewing crude patches on them, and finding an old felt hat you could poke full of holes. If you had an old pair of boots with soles that flapped as you walked, that was good too.

Besides the costumes, the distinguishing characteristic of the Sadie Hawkins dance was that the girls had to ask the boys. Normally, it was taboo for a girl to ask a boy to a dance or a movie or anywhere else. Girls who did were considered cheap and forward and easy and would end up as unwed mothers or in the Yale Repertory Theatre. But on Sadie Hawkins Day the girls could escape the societal straitjacket that had been prepared for them.

It was a time when lots of couples broke up, because it was easier for a girl to put up with a boyfriend until she could ask someone else to the Sadie Hawkins dance than it was to articulate all the delicate reasons she didn't want to go steady with him anymore. The girls put lots of effort into decorating the gym for the dance. It was a big deal for them.

Nobody asked me to the dance. The boys who did get asked all had cars. None of them was socially inept.

Down the valley from Hailey was Bellevue, and Bellevue was even poorer than Hailey. Kids from Bellevue didn't have to search through boxes of old clothes to find a costume for the Sadie Hawkins dance. Those of us from Hailey held ourselves above our classmates from Bellevue. We had learned this sort of behavior from our classmates up the valley in Ketchum and Sun Valley, who held themselves above us.

Below Bellevue is an agricultural area known as Poverty Flats. Today it's an area of white-fenced horse pastures and riding stables and big houses, but then it was full of starve-acre farms growing hay or barley. It had been the location of the county poor farm during the Great Depression, and the local joke was that the soil was so poor there that even the poor farm couldn't make it.

Kids from Bellevue held themselves above kids from Poverty Flats. And the poorest of the poor kids from Poverty Flats, the person that even the kids from Poverty Flats held themselves above, was in my class. His name was Eddy Casto. And he was even more socially inept than I was, because when the Sadie Hawkins dance came around that fall, he went by himself.

No one in our collective memory had ever gone to a Sadie Hawkins dance alone. If you were a girl, you didn't go alone to Sadie Hawkins because that meant everyone you had asked had turned you down. If you were a boy, you didn't go alone because that meant no one had asked you.

Eddy Casto wore a belt that was cinched too tight, with a big nickel-silver buckle with a stamped-steel horse head riveted to it, and dirty white high-rise denim jeans and boots that were like cowboy boots except the tops ended at his ankles. His hair was ill-cut and stiff with Brylcreem. He wore a wrinkled cowboy shirt with tattered piping and glasses that made his eyes look huge and loose in their sockets. That is the way I remember him, and that is the outfit he wore when he went alone to the Sadie Hawkins dance.

Here is what I was told happened: nobody paid much attention to Eddy for half the dance. He hung around the punchbowl and talked to the ancient teachers who were the chaperones. He didn't dance with anyone because everyone else was part of a couple.

But after an hour or so, Eddy started trying to cut in on the dancers, who told him to go away, mostly, or cut right back in a minute later and then told him to go away. Finally he got angry, and went to a corner of the gym and found a broom. He walked it out to the center of the floor and began to dance with it.

After a while a few people turned to watch him. They began pointing and whispering, and more people began to watch, and finally everybody at the dance, ragged in their Sadie Hawkins clothes, formed a great circle around him and began clapping and chanting his name in time to the music.

Eddy began jumping high and spinning, swinging the broom around in a wide circle, holding it between his legs and riding it like a hobby horse, and finally holding it above his head, all the while high-kicking and throwing his free arm out in a spastic parody of dance, and making a high mewling noise through his clenched teeth. "Eddy Casto!" everyone shouted. "Eddy Casto! Eddy Casto!" Finally the ancient chaperones noticed what was going on, cut the music, and made Eddy go home.

I heard that the rest of the dance was pretty good. People loosened up and started making moves that they'd only practiced once or twice in front of the mirrors in their bedrooms.

The next Monday Eddy Casto showed up in school wearing the same clothes, acting like nothing had happened. Everybody else acted like nothing had happened, but after I heard the story I couldn't bear to look at him. If he sat down next to me in study hall I moved across the room, just in case he started to make that awful mewling noise.

Late that fall our drama department staged an adaptation of Shirley Jackson's short story, "The Lottery," and I had a role as one of the townspeople in the last scene, where the winner of the lottery is ritually stoned to death. We had spray painted a hundred or so sponges grey for the stones, and in dress rehearsal, as I picked up my three or four sponges to throw at the girl who was playing the sacrificial victim, I looked at her and realized I hated her.

When the time came, I threw my sponges with all my heart. I noticed that I wasn't the only one who was throwing hard. Our victim collapsed under a pile of bouncing sponges. The drama teacher made us stop and said that the bouncing sponges were an unintended sight gag and we should throw more softly. The girl playing the lead drew praise for her screams and cries. "Nobody could tell you didn't think you really were going to die," said the teacher.

Until that moment I had liked the girl playing the female lead. I had fantasized that someday she would ask me to the Sadie Hawkins dance.

After the play was over I got enough courage to ask her out. But on our date the memory of the hate I had felt for her in the play came back and I couldn't look at her. We watched a bad movie and I took her home and didn't kiss her goodnight. I don't remember anything else we said or did.

LET'S LOOK back at my edit of *The Little Match Girl*.

What's surprising about a version of a story where three-fourths of the original has been edited out is how much survives, either as the story or as its shadow. The idea of the excised parts of a story retaining a ghostly existence is valid if you imagine the animators working on the Disney version of *The Little Match Girl* using my edited version as their script. Everything they need is there. Of course, these are people experienced in taking words and using them to create a rich visual tapestry, filling in details with their imaginations, discovering things that neither author nor editor could imagine. In other words, they are the kind of readers you hope connect with your writing.

Also surprising is that the architecture of the story survives just fine. The cold and the dark start the conflict. The intensity rises when the girl appears, rises higher with her hunger and the smell of roast goose, higher with the subjunctive appearance of her abusive father, and higher still with each match that is burnt, until an overwhelming vision, one which equates death with salvation, ends the conflict.

Look at the elements of the story that made the cut. There is the Little Match Girl, her abusive father, a walking cooked goose, a grandmother who is dead, the same grandmother come back to life, and God, who appears in both versions as a where and not a who, which throws the light of geography on the problem of human suffering in this universe. And there are the passersby, who appear as witnesses.

When you have a witness you have a point-of-view shift, from narrative character to the story itself. We thought we were seeing things from the Little Match Girl's point-of-view, but when the witnesses see her but fail to comprehend the truth, there is an immediate shift to the point-of-view of the story.

But that's not all. Earlier there were some other more subtle violations of points-of-view, the first when the father appears in the subjunctive and not the indicative. Then the stone wall the Little Match Girl leans against disappears and she hallucinates a stove and a food-laden table and a Christmas tree. Then the Christmas tree fades and its candles are revealed to be stars. We see all of these as expansions in the awareness of the Little Match Girl, but from the reader's standpoint, they act as a movie camera pulling away from her to show us the father, the rich tables and warm stoves and well-decorated trees inside the houses, and finally the stars.

There is one more point-of-view change. It occurs when the story gives itself to the reader. Those of us who bridle against the restrictiveness of the point-of-view rule can console ourselves with the idea that every story's final line shifts the entire story into the reader's point-of-view, in this case the reader who has seen the visions in the match flames, who now knows God is a where and not a who, and who waits for the next story.

I'M USING a different metaphor here than I began with. The writer as Little Match Girl has been changed to the writer as *The Little Match Girl*—the writer as the story. It's a much less reductive metaphor, and it allows for *outsight* without the pain of being an outsider. When James Castle's gallery sells one of his drawings for twenty thousand dollars, I don't wish I were he, no matter how rich and full his inner universe is. If Eddy Casto had become an Oscar-winning choreographer, I would have run screaming from an invitation to his post-Academy Awards party and dance. If the price of creating outsider art is being an Outsider, the price is too high.

But if the price of writing a story is losing one's self and becoming the story, and as the story, turning toward your readers, it *is* worth it. The metaphor is messy and full of loose ends, but that only means it's moving in the right direction, away from neatness and toward complexity and paradox and even ritual.

A person as a sequence of stories doesn't do much for our concept of ourselves as autonomous individuals. But when we meet someone new, we might ask our friends, "What's his story?" When we want to understand the contradictions in someone we're close to, we ask, "What's your story?" In moments of profound self-reflection we might ask, "What's my story?"

It's a giddy and not entirely comfortable feeling when you're writing a story and you reach that point of concentration where you dissolve into the words. It's a kind of death, or at least the death of that thing you mean when you write the capital letter I on a page. You've stared into flames long enough that the visions appear, sharp-edged and impossibly bright, and they become so much of the world that you forget point-of-view entirely, because the view has obliterated the viewer.

That's what you want to happen when you write, but it's never what the person you call "I" will want. There will always be a fight for existence between you and your story.

We know from various biographers that Hans Christian Andersen felt like an outsider all of his life, even after he was declared a national treasure and given a lifetime stipend by the King of Denmark.

But if he started this story out of a place of damage and grief, there must have come a point, writing along, working on the bones of his story, when the writing took over. In a cold room, he must have felt a great warmth. It appeared in his vision as a stove. He must have felt a wealth of words if nothing else, which appeared as a table laden with food and a walking roast goose. If his room had a window he must have seen in the whole world a great and temporary starlit beauty, which appeared to him as a Christmas tree full of candles. He must have understood his insignificance in the universe but he also must have understood that his insignificance allowed him to *see* the universe. Seeing the universe, he must have intuited a place free from hunger and cold and fear, which let him approach God. He must have realized that the Little Match Girl—that frozen outsider that he saw himself as—was not *all* that he was. He must have realized what he was doing was ritual, ritual carried to the level of magic. He must have shimmered, grown transparent, and disappeared, leaving a story in his place.

Rules for Writers

Eddy Casto's Ten Suggestions for Going to the Writer's Ball Alone

1. Don't go alone. Take your reader with you. Otherwise you can get caught up in the grotesque choreography of solipsism.

2. Writing is co-written. The common name for co-author is reader.

3. Skilled readers make you a better writer, even when the words stay the same. To the extent that you can select or attract skilled readers, you're like a playwright casting his own play.

4. Your reader ends the story gazing at the story. The gaze of the story is always back toward the reader. Try not to get between them, or you'll spoil the romance.

5. Stand outside of comfortable and happy insiders, but stand outside of outsiders as well. Work to achieve the consciousness of the story and not the author.

6. If these concepts are difficult and painful and don't yield immediately to your understanding, things could be worse. Imagine what it would be like to go through life as Eddy Casto. Imagine being Eddy Casto and putting down your broom, leaving the dance, and going home to Poverty Flats to work until dawn on your novel.

7. At some point in the writing of a story, the author and the story will be like predatory twins in a womb, trying to

cannibalize each other for nutrients. (Maybe now you can see why I have trouble with metaphors.)

8. All great writers understand their insignificance, which allows them to escape the tight first-person point-of-view of their lives.

9. There is plenty of loneliness in the world. It's not a requirement that you be lonely or alienated to write. At some point in the writing of every story, loneliness and alienation will take care of themselves and threaten to take care of you.

10. Having relationships characterized by loyalty and humor and fidelity and honesty and depth is not a requirement for being a writer. It is a requirement for being a *happy* writer.

3

Writing Shadows

How shall I save my light through this long twilight?
—Friedrich Nietzsche

I'LL BEGIN with a past-life regression. In this case, the past life is my own. It occurred in 1955, in Hailey, Idaho. But before I get to my own story, let me tell you a little about the poet Ezra Pound.

Hailey is famous in literary circles as Pound's birthplace. Pound founded the poetic movement known as imagism, and was a defining voice in the broader cultural movement known as modernism. He wrote *The Cantos,* an epic poem that stands as his life's work, much in the way that *Leaves of Grass* stands as Walt Whitman's life's work. Pound's most famous work, however, is the editing job he did for T.S. Eliot, shaping *The Waste Land* into the great canonical poem of the twentieth century.

Pound wrote essays about writing, and wrote them so well that if a teacher ever gave you writing advice like Show Don't Tell or Use The Least Amount of Words for the Most Amount of Meaning, you can assume Pound said it first and said it better and said it with more urgency.

Besides Eliot, Pound knew and influenced Robert Frost,

Ernest Hemingway, Marianne Moore, William Carlos Williams, Gertrude Stein, James Joyce, and William Butler Yeats. He dominated the literary conversation of the early twentieth century by intelligence, talent, and force of personality.

Pound didn't dominate anything while he was in Hailey. His parents moved to Philadelphia in 1887 when he was two. Even if he had wanted to stay and work in central Idaho's mines instead of becoming a successful poet and Nazi cheerleader, he yet lacked the words to mount an effective argument for a dangerous and ill-paid life underground.

It's difficult to remember things that happened to you when you were two, but a small hint of Pound's life in Hailey can be detected in *The Cantos*. Here are three lines from "The Garden," from 1916, the most fatal year of the First World War:

> And round about there is a rabble
> Of the filthy, sturdy, unkillable infants of the very poor.
> They shall inherit the earth.

Pound was not thinking of the Belgian trenches, where those filthy sturdy infants were dying by the millions after being ordered by their officers over the ramparts and into machine-gun fire. I suggest that he was instead thinking about his birthplace, where, for a while, those infants did live to inherit the earth, at least the mined-out, falling-down, starve-acre part of it that was the town of Hailey.

I was one of those infants. My father was one of the men who went down in the mines that lay beneath Idaho's sagebrush-covered hills. He met my mother in the winter of 1940, at a dance eleven miles north of Hailey in the resort town of Ketchum, famous in literary circles as the location of Ernest Hemingway's 1961 death-by-shotgun. My mother was a nurse at the Hailey Hospital, but by the time I was born in 1950 she was working as a nurse at the Sun Valley Resort, where the wages were marginally better and the patients were mostly young and sprained, instead of crushed by rockfall in the mines or riven with silicosis or cirrhosis. Our family was living in company housing at the Triumph Mine on the East Fork of the Wood River, halfway between Hailey and Ketchum. In literary terms, my life fell midway between the birthplace of a fascist and the killing ground of a suicide.

In 1957, two years after the past-life I've promised to begin with, the mayor of Hailey wrote to Ezra Pound in Washington, D.C., at St. Elizabeth's Hospital for the criminally insane, where Pound had been confined since his 1945 arrest for treason. Due to his aid and comfort to the enemy, and the release of photos and stories of the death factories of Hitler's empire, he would have been hung if he hadn't been declared mad. But the Hailey mayor, sensing Pound's imminent return to sanity and consequent release, invited him back to his birthplace for the seventy-fifth anniversary of the town's founding. They declared him a native son and invited him home to what honors a town of sturdy unkillables could provide.

Pound wrote back to the effect that if he could have left the Godforsaken town of Hailey in the Godforsaken state of Idaho even before his birth, he would have.

Shortly thereafter, his rehabilitation complete, Pound left for Venice where he gave the fascist salute to reporters on his arrival and lived in a grumpy and regret-stained *ménage a trois* with his wife and mistress until his death at age 87 in 1972.

A past-life regression? More like a past-life *di*gression so far, you're thinking, and yet 1916 and 1955 and Ezra Pound are a way of talking around a morale-killing question for writers: how do we find the will to write even a word, considering that the man who did so much to define our language and its literary structures went on to use his talent to cheer on murderers in death camps? For those of us staring at an empty screen, the idea that beauty can come out of evil is a threat, and the idea that a human being can be capable of beauty and at the same time have a moral vacuum at his core is a worse threat.

But just as Hemingway's blood lay on the linoleum in patterns that showed the empty, clean place where his body had fallen, it might be possible to learn about that nothingness by looking at what lies at its edges.

IN THE FALL OF 1955 I was five years old. My father had quit the mines and was working as a ski bus driver for the Sun Valley Resort in the winter and spring, and as a trapper and a fishing and hunting guide in the summer and fall.

We had also moved from the Triumph Mine company town to Hailey. My brother was in school, but I had to stay with a sitter during the days.

The person my parents hired to care for me was a desperate housewife before desperate housewives were even remotely interesting. She was the young wife of one of my father's colleagues at the bus garage, and she had three children under four, and even now I can remember her screaming at them when they got too loud or when the television didn't work. The television often didn't work because the reception from southern Idaho stations was a matter of the right configuration of clouds and sun and ozone.

When she went shopping at the Hailey Mercantile, she locked her children and me in a car that had the lock posts removed. When lock posts were unscrewed from their internal mechanisms, it became impossible to unlock the doors from inside the car. It was a way to use cars as portable pens for small children, although you had to leave the windows open a crack in the summer or they'd die on you.

But when she left us there in the car and disappeared into the Mercantile, we would scream and cry and honk the horn until she would come raging out of the store, unlock a door, grab one of her kids and pound on it until the crying and the screaming and the honking stopped. Then she'd throw the kid back in, lock the door and disappear. I don't remember that she bought much, but she had a rudimentary sense of guilt that had her bringing candy or ice cream bars out of the store on the days when she had beat one of her kids.

She only hit me once. It was a solid slap across the face that sent me to the floor. It was in early December of 1955, and I had been talking with my brother, and he had told me that Santa Claus didn't exist. Santa Claus wasn't a generous old guy with a big white beard in a red and white suit. Santa Claus was really your parents sneaking in an extra gift for you.

I told this to my sitter's oldest child, and he told the others. They all started crying and then the sitter started crying and then she hit me. She was a big woman and I was a little five-year-old kid, but I never told my parents what had happened because I assumed that I had done something wrong. I kept staying at my sitter's house until that spring, when my grandmother, with whom I had stayed on occasion, agreed to watch me on a regular basis.

Anyway, I *had* done something wrong.

On one of the days that fall when the television worked, the newscast contained an announcement that the Soviet Union had tested a hydrogen bomb. It was on a date made ironic by subsequent events: November 22, 1955. My sitter reacted violently—cursing or crying loudly enough that I asked her what was wrong.

"The Russians are going to kill us," she said.

I asked her how they were going to do that. She told me about the bomb.

I knew what a bomb was, having seen them on TV during one of the TV's good days. They were big black balls with fuses that blew up evil cartoon characters, cats mostly.

"I could stop the bomb," I said. "I'd get a knife and cut the fuse."

"It doesn't have a fuse," she said. "It has a big electrical cable instead of a fuse."

"Then before it blew up," I said, "I'd cut the cable with a cable cutter." My imaginary version of the H-bomb—and hers, come to think of it—just sat there for a while before blowing up, long enough to tinker with. My father had welding equipment in his shop and I was thinking of his cutting torch, which he had allowed me to watch through the dark lens of his welding hood.

I remember her exact reply: "How could you cut the cable of a bomb that's bigger than this house?"

I had a sudden vision of electrical cable as thick as the neck of a horse. I decided to try a different tack. "They wouldn't bomb Hailey," I said. "They'd bomb Sun Valley."

Even as a five-year-old, I had an inkling that the rich people in Sun Valley were more likely to be a target of the Soviets than the poor people of Hailey.

My sitter looked at me, a kind of perverse triumph in her eyes. "If they bomb Sun Valley, the explosion will be so big that we'll die too, only a little later than my husband and your mother and father."

I stopped arguing with her.

How do you bring more torment into the life of a woman whose life is already brimming with torment? You take a position in her house as the oldest person available for conversation, and then when she wants to talk about her fears of dying in a nuclear war between competing ideologies she doesn't understand, you don't offer her any viable solutions. You try, but your solutions are so pathetic, so cartoon-like, so lacking of understanding of the real situation that even she realizes that you're only five years old. And then you tell her that Santa Claus doesn't exist.

THAT'S MY PAST-LIFE regression. One of the problems with past-life regressions is that they're embarrassing. It's a kind of sifting through heaps of your own love letters to people who dumped you and things you wrote in yearbooks and garbage full of empty half-gallon bottles of Gallo Hearty Burgundy and Pop-Tarts wrappers.

In a 1904 essay on the nature of history, Bertrand Russell wrote: "The past alone is truly real: the present is but a painful struggling birth into the immutable being of what is no longer."

But Russell went on to live long enough to know that the past can be painful, too, and that the present achieves a kind of immutable being through embarrassment. If I could change the past so it were less embarrassing, my present would be less substantial than it is, because I would have had no need to develop the sort of moral heft that lets me live with shame. It's occurred to me that Ezra Pound's lack of moral heft might be related to his lack of shame.

I kept the name of my sitter just below the threshold of consciousness for most of fifty years, until a few years back when it jumped at me from the obituary column of the *Wood River Journal*, the weekly Hailey paper. She had died of some dread long-term curse like lupus or Lou Gehrig's Disease or one of the other physical horrors that make you think that when God got through with Job he wasn't through with the rest of us. The picture published with her obituary showed her in a terrible state of obesity and inflammation.

I looked further through the paper. I scan it now for the mere mention of a familiar person or family name, as Sun Valley has indeed exploded south and almost all the people I grew up with in Hailey are gone, pushed out by gentrification. They've been replaced by immigrants from a land where money is a plentiful commodity instead of a measure of sweat and tears. They're Lycra-clad cross-training money managers and plastic surgeons and lawyers and venture capitalists and landscapers and headhunters and people who shorted the market in 2008.

In that same issue of the paper, one of my dead sitter's grandsons had gotten caught in his car with an ounce of meth sitting on the console between himself and his girlfriend, who

was herself the spawn of those new people, the ones who pur-
chased Hailey from those filthy sturdy unkillable poor folks
whose birthright it was.

So maybe one of the embarrassing things about being a five-
year-old in this woman's house was that I didn't realize she was
going to die horribly or that her family was going to have to
move because they were poor. Maybe the H-bomb was the least
of her worries. One of the shameful things about who I am now
is that when I saw that obituary, I didn't feel pity so much as a
grim satisfaction that the person who had made my life miserable for a few months when I was five had gotten hers.

Last year I gave a reading to creative writing students in the
Hailey high school and afterward found the room where they
keep all the old yearbooks. I discovered my sitter's picture as a
high-school senior in 1951. She had been beautiful and young
and intelligent once. When I knew her she was fifty or sixty
pounds heavier and four years older with three screaming kids
and not enough money. She was no longer beautiful and no longer young, and was systematically killing her own intelligence
because she couldn't see any way out of the fix she was in. Consciousness in that situation is just another burden.

WILLIAM GOLDING in his autobiographical novel *Free Fall*
charges himself with the task of finding out that point in his life
when he lost his free will, the ability to choose or even influence his own destiny. For my sitter, that point must have come
when she was about eighteen. For the nation she grew up in,
that point must have come right around the time they put Ezra
Pound in St. Elizabeth's Hospital instead of killing him. That

was when the Alamogordo desert lit up like a neon sign and Robert Oppenheimer quoted from the *Bhagavad-Gita*:

> If the radiance of a thousand suns
> Were to burst at once into the sky
> That would be like the splendor of the mighty one.
> I am become Death
> The shatterer of worlds.

People believed in the *Bhagavad-Gita* in 1955. When I got to my grandmother's house she spent long hours explaining H-bombs to me and showing me the routes the Russian bombers would take across Santa Claus's home.

I'M APPROACHING these subjects through story because that's the best way to explain things to writers. I have told writers that the current night-sea journey of our culture, a journey of great danger that we must endure with great loneliness, is the experience of nihilism. It's waking up at four A.M. in the midst of dark grey shapes in a dimly lit world where God has crumbled to dust and intimacy only exists as autonomic reflex.

I've gone further to say that nihilism cannot be avoided. If you avoid it, you start lying to the people who read your words. Keep it up and you'll eventually start lying to yourself and you wake up at four A.M. anyway, but this time as an inarticulate and uncomprehending and tormented animal.

I say this as if I've conquered nihilism. I say it as if I've staked out a section in that green valley that lies just over the summit from the Valley of Death, and it's the Promised Land, happily cleared of its previous inhabitants by bird flu or smallpox. There's clean water in the creek that flows through the place, and due to global warming the frost goes out of the ground in February, and there are apples and chokecherries on the trees, camas in the meadows, and venison in the old-growth forest just behind the homestead cabin.

I tell people to go through nihilism, as if I've escaped a soulless market-run scientific material culture. I say it as if I'm safely divorced from Hailey, Idaho, now a ghetto of extreme wealth, where vacant-eyed Hummer-drivers are building houses that cost the dollar equivalent of forty-five Habitat for Humanity homes and venture capital is building great state-of-the-art hospitals for a community of ten thousand. I see house lots selling for two million dollars, and bus drivers and nurses and maids and gardeners and mechanics and grocery clerks exiled sixty or a hundred miles south. They commute to work for a community that will not build low-cost housing because it would depress property values.

I say go through nihilism, as if I can no longer see politicians at press conferences, pretending a foolish literalism in the face of questions of conscience. I say go through nihilism as if I cannot see the grinning skulls beneath those sheaths of skin. Then I see other grinning skulls conducting suicide bombings for the perverse promise of being able to live in Paradise—as if questions of conscience don't exist in Paradise—and the grinning skull of an eerily reincarnated Pope, the grinning skulls of senators explaining the will of the American people and the endless grinning skulls in that shock-of-recognition apocalyptic nightmare that has been the backdrop of *The Terminator* movies.

And then I realize that I'm still in the Valley of Death. I

haven't escaped these things. I haven't gotten through nihilism. I'm in it. I was drinking at a wine bar in Hailey just the other day.

So maybe you'd think that I'd start telling new writers to stay away from nihilism, to find meaning in hunting-and-gathering at big box stores, or in having kids and in going to church or playing in a city soccer league or building an eight thousand square foot house. But I can't tell that to anyone and keep a straight face, not even if I'm talking to a writer.

Writing moves you toward a consciousness of everyday life as being just the surface layer of froth on a dark sea of reality. And once under the surface, you discover that your scuba tanks are full of nothing. You can try to breathe it, but it will end up breathing you.

I'LL TRY to make up for that last metaphor by telling another story.

I went to high school with a guy named Kenny Rivers. His father, Joe Rivers, was a good and profane friend of my father's. Joe's wife was Mary, who belonged to a religious group called the Followers of Christ. The Followers believed that modern medicine violated God's will. God was in charge of sickness and would bring health if He felt like it. Doctors, who dared to thwart God's plan, were in league with Satan.

I don't know how Joe and Mary got together, but their marriage was one of those where the wife remained in her faith and prayed for the husband's soul and the husband drank and gambled and stayed out late and in general assumed that his wife's prayers would be successful without much cooperation on his part.

They had two girls and Kenny, and Mary's father, their

grandfather, insisted that they be raised in the faith. Then the girls both died of appendicitis in the midst of prayer sessions, a year apart. When Joe tried to take the second girl to the hospital for an appendectomy, Mary's father stood in the doorway and would not let him pass.

A few years later, Kenny came down with appendicitis and when Mary got on the phone to her father for a prayer session, Joe put the boy in the car and took him to the Hailey Hospital. When the old man and a few of the Follower faithful came to the hospital to take the boy back home, Joe blew out the windshield of Mary's father's car with a shotgun. Then he told them to leave and they did, prayer having been less than effective against military force since the time of the Albigensians and before.

So Kenny was an only child when I went to high school with him, but he was a living one.

There's a twist to this story. Mary's father, familiar by this time with the symptoms of appendicitis, one day discovered them in himself and disappeared. Mary found him recovering from surgery in a hospital in Salt Lake City, where he had checked himself in.

Mary, still a true believer, died of untreated cancer. Joe and Kenny stopped following Christ if they ever had. I don't know what happened to the old man but he's either dead now or God in his mercy might have seen to it that he has been kept going for the last fifty years by means of a feeding tube and respirator.

One moral of this story might be that if God really wants you to die you get something that doctors can't cure. But another is that even people who profess to believe in the immortal soul are scientific materialists at heart. The hypocrisy of Mary's father might be extreme, but it isn't unfamiliar.

Almost anyone who has pondered scientific materialism has discovered that at its objective heart is a void that will swallow up every human dignity, every religious yearning, every thought of honor and virtue and beauty and compassion in the world. But that doesn't stop people from worshipping it in practice even as they scorn it in principle. Medical insurance takes up a larger and larger portion of our national wealth, even though what it guarantees for almost half of its beneficiaries is a longer, more painful, less dignified and lonelier death.

But I have seen my own undergraduate students go happily off to medical school, full of hope and idealism and a plan to make the world a less diseased and less tragic place. I see them eight years later and their most fervent faith is in the God of Malpractice Insurance. When the high priests of scientific materialism lose their faith, we should start looking around for another game in town. But most of us will stick with what we can see, and what we can see is doctors and hospitals and tests and procedures.

Mary's father must have felt his own swollen abdomen and suddenly understood what it must have been like to be Christ in Gethsemane, and left one faith for another.

THE IDAHO WRITER Vardis Fisher wrote a massive book called *Orphans in Gethsemane*, which was his autobiography. The last quarter of it details his intellectual quest for meaning in a God-forsaken world. He found it in a kind of good-hearted American pragmatism and empiricism—the Cyrus McCormick/Orville Wright/Milton Friedman/Thomas Edison end of scientific materialism—but toward the end of his life he quite pragmatically and empirically drank himself to death.

This Godforsaken-ness that Vardis Fisher failed to overcome isn't a recent phenomenon, although Nietzsche and World War I, the Holocaust, the rise of Orwell's bureaucratic nightmare, the A-bomb, the H-bomb, nerve gas and weaponized smallpox have given the current void a recognizable shape.

The same void is there in Job and Homer and Sophocles. Shakespeare has Richard III and Prince Hamlet and Lear raging on the heath. Here's William Blake, addressing God, or what he can sense of God, in his poem "To Nobodaddy":

> Why art thou silent and invisible
> Father of jealousy
> Why dost thou hide thyself in clouds
> From every searching Eye
>
> Why darkness and obscurity
> In all thy words and laws
> That none dare eat the fruit but from
> The wily serpent's jaws

The best part of that poem is its title. Nobodaddy's still around. Sylvia Plath had a Nobodaddy. Job had a Nobodaddy.

In the story of Job, we have this passage:

> ...on the day when the angels come to testify before the Lord, the accusing Angel [Satan] came too.
> The Lord said to the Accuser, "Where have you come from?"

The Accuser answered, "From walking here and there on the earth, and looking around."

The Lord said, "Did you notice my servant Job? There is no one on earth like him: a man of perfect integrity, who fears God and avoids evil. He is holding on to his innocence, even after you made me torment him for no reason."

The Accuser said, "So what? A man will give up everything he has to save his own skin. But just reach out and strike his flesh and bones, and I bet he'll curse you to your face."

The Lord said, "All right: he is in your power."

That last line contains the shock of recognition. We don't see God, but we can infer his existence from the prisoner renditions.

NOTHINGNESS. It's what's for breakfast at the writer's table.

Dostoevsky gives us murderers, child molesters, suicides, and devilish compulsions. Kierkegaard gives us fear and loathing unto death. Camus begins *The Myth of Sisyphus* with the sentence that there is but one truly serious philosophical problem, and that is suicide. Faulkner gives us the psychopath Popeye and the ratlike Snopeses and Miss Emily for a lover. Robert Penn Warren, in his anatomy of the human heart called *All the King's Men*, gives us the Big Twitch, a mindless reflex that passes for human connection in Louisiana and elsewhere. Hemingway gives us *Our Nada Who Art In Nada*. Margaret Atwood gives us Bluebeard as husband. Fitzgerald gives us the soul of Gatsby twining with the souls of Daisy and Tom Buchanan, and we watch as all those souls evaporate before our eyes. Eliot, after showing us John Webster's skull beneath the skin, asks us to warm our metaphysics against breastless ribs. Ralph Ellison gives us an invisible man who lives in a room lined with bright-lit bulbs just so he can see enough of himself to believe in his own existence.

NO WONDER the surgeon's son Foucault, who gives us a vision of our world as history's prison and our social relationships as psychic cannibalism, is not so much philosopher but Philosopher's Stone, the irreducible final substance that transforms whatever it touches. In his analyses of bondage and torture, in his delicate tracings of power relationships, in his simultaneous HIV positivity and promiscuity, in his chrome-skulled leather-clad shimmering between rage and reason, he gives us a final vision of what it is to evolve beyond the human.

JORGE LUIS BORGES, in his great short story "The Garden of the Forking Paths," indicates that you cannot escape a labyrinth by going forward. Escape is behind you. So in my attempt to find a reason to write in the face of Foucault and his precursors, I'd like to visit Stockholm on December 10, 1950: William Faulkner's Nobel Prize acceptance speech.

Faulkner says the reason for his life's work is "to create out of the materials of the human spirit something which did not exist before." But then he discusses writing in the face of an overwhelming question: When will I be blown up?

Because of this question, Faulkner says, "The young man or woman writing today has forgotten the problems of the human heart in conflict with itself which alone can make good writing because only that is worth…the agony and the sweat."

Writers, Faulkner says, "must teach [themselves] that the

basest of all things is to be afraid…and then forget [fear] forever, leaving no room…for anything but the old verities and truths of the heart…love and honor and pity and pride and compassion and sacrifice." Until they do that, he says, their griefs will leave no scars.

Faulkner says the writer's duty is to delve deep into grief and scars, in order to lift humanity's collective heart. He says the writer needs to remind readers of the courage and honor and hope and pride and compassion and pity and sacrifice that are the glories of our birthright.

There might be something in the Stockholm water, because here is an excerpt from John Steinbeck's Nobel Prize acceptance speech twelve years later:

"The writer is delegated to declare and to celebrate humanity's proven capacity for greatness of heart and spirit—for gallantry in defeat, for courage, compassion, and love. In the endless war against weakness and despair, these are the bright rally flags of hope and of emulation."

Of course, Hemingway, in his Nobel Prize speech in 1954, wrote "The writer works alone and must face eternity or the lack of it every day," which is a less hopeful thought. But he wasn't there in Stockholm to drink the water, having been injured in two consecutive airplane rides that ended in crashes a few months before.

I do think, and maybe Hemingway's example supports the idea, that if you stop believing in hope, nihilism is much harder to face. You might think that nihilism and hope are contradictions in terms. But lots of contradictory concepts, once they're embodied in the physical world, exist quite happily together, sometimes in the same object. The empty screen that we writers face every time we sit down to write is both nothingness and hope.

It's a dangerous combination, but it's *our* combination.

THERE IS A BRONZE PLAQUE on the Hailey house where Ezra Pound was born. It was put there by an Irish theater director in 1986. He was in Sun Valley to direct Yale drama students during their summer retreat. He explained to the people of the Wood River Valley that although Pound was a man who had given aid and comfort to the enemy, we shouldn't hold that against him. We should instead honor Pound as a man who had shaped our literature and by extension, shaped our selves. No doubt we should also have bronze plaques for the birthplaces of Edward Teller and Joseph McCarthy and Robert MacNamara, other shapers of our selves.

There is evidence that Pound may have come to some late awareness of the evil he had done. In a 1967 interview, he told Allen Ginsberg that he had discovered he had spent his life not as a lunatic but as a moron, and in a more resonant statement, said this: "The intention was bad—that's the trouble—anything [good] I've done has been an accident—any good has been spoiled by my intentions..."

IN THOSE WORDS, we get a hint of that moment when Pound lost his free will by deciding he was in control of his writing. He replaced serendipity with intentionality. Such moments bid us to back further out of Borges' labyrinth. Pound, in those years from 1958 to 1972, was a once-bright ember slowly fading behind a thickening layer of ash. None of us with a writing life would want to end ours the way his ended.

It may be that none of us who write want our lives to end at all—that's what the books are all about—and yet a writing life takes us to those depths where we contemplate our own end. What poem or story isn't a *memento mori,* at least if you listen to the writing advisor who is incessantly urging you to *go deeper?* Break through that glass bottom of your ocean. Board that ship for your night-sea journey. Walk through the portal that leads to the Valley of Death. Hope you make it back.

AND YET it's good advice. The soil in the Valley of Death is deep and fertile. The climate is mild. And there's light there, even if the way many people have described it is as paradox: brightness born of the dark, darkness visible, images outlined by a hallucinatory glittering blackness—a blackness that always causes a shock of recognition. The way Pound put it in one of the Cantos was "beasts like shadows in the glass."

That's not a daylit image, but it does produce its own kind of light. When I think of Ezra Pound as a glowing ember, I think that as a young man he must have seen in himself a dark fire capable of blinding petty intention, and as long as he could see by it and see what it demanded of him he could avoid the mundane intention that ruined anything good he ever did.

He must have backed out of the Valley of Death into ordinary daylight. On some deep level, he must have lost his nerve to go where bigger things than his own great ego lurked in the shadows.

The Valley of Death is the giant warehouse of broken statues, the prop-room for a closed theater, the abandoned city, the organ bank, the pottery shards, the medicine bundle, the ship-breaker's beach, the caves overlooking the Dead Sea, the deceased collector's display room. It's your writer's inheritance, one that will claim you as strongly as you dare claim it.

ONE WAY of being true to yourself as a writer is by cleaving to the image. Cleaving to the image means just what it says: sticking with it and simultaneously being separate from it, object to its subject. There's a humility to this way of looking at things that lasts only until we decide that an image stands for something else. That's when it becomes part of our conscious intention and we not only lose our humility, we lose the image.

I owe thanks not to Ezra Pound but to James Hillman, the depth psychologist, for this way of looking at image. Hillman wrote a good book called *Suicide and the Soul*, which postulates the idea that the needs of the soul are much different from those of the body or those of the intellect. Hillman says we subsume soul into intellect in our culture—that's the sort of thing that has us giving doctors the position of priests—so when we pay lip service to life after death we're confusing our soul with our conscious identity. That's not giving the soul its due.

Hillman says that in the extreme, the soul reclaims its own by violence, which is what sadism and suicide are all about.

In another good book called *Dream and the Underworld*, Hillman states that our daylit life is only a perverse parody of our reality, which lies in the images of our dreams.

Moreover, those images contain imperatives. Images embody a morality. Images contain whole poems, stories, and books. Faulkner found *The Sound and the Fury* in the eidetic memory of a little girl's muddy underwear.

Hillman says that soul makes its home close to the image, but the soul will flee the image if you analyze it. Our dreams are full of soul until we decide what they mean.

There must have been a point at which Ezra Pound's soul fled his intellect, and certainly a point at which he lost the ability to back out of the labyrinth of his life. Yet if you look at Robert Creeley, a poet deeply influenced by Pound, you see someone whose soul remained undiminished throughout his life, a poet who kept returning to the image and doing what it told him to do.

You may notice that when I write about a soul-killing culture, it's easy to agree with me but when I write about real souls—maybe even your soul—your intellect takes over and enforces a certain precautionary distance from, for example, the idea that the image of *beasts like shadows in the glass* has anything to do with you. But look at Robert Creeley's poem "A Wicker Basket." It's a soul-image—a sturdy woven place he goes to when "it's later/and onto your table the headwaiter/puts the bill," and from the comfort of which he can see

> very huge stars, man, in the sky
> and from somewhere very far off someone hands me a slice of
> apple pie
> with a gob of white, white ice cream on top of it,
> and I eat it—
> Slowly. And while certainly
> they are laughing at me, and all around me is racket
> of these cats not making it, I make it
> in my wicker basket.

Even if you can't believe in the soul you can believe in the image, and its imperative of accepting the apple pie and the white, white ice cream when it's handed to you. Maybe Pound in his arrogant intentionality lost the ability to accept images on their own generous terms, and thus lost his soul. Hillman gives many definitions for the soul but one that I like is that the soul is the active interface between self and image.

Substitute story for soul and you can see that writing a story or poem requires an image, too. Writing requires perceiving something and trying to fit words to it, then looking again and writing the words the second look gives you, and continuing this process until you're done.

What you will have gained in that exercise is more than a story or poem. You will have gained a world full of something-ness. You will have gained a sense that all your art is *found art*. The moments when you find an image that sticks with you are lucky moments indeed. Taking what you find and doing what you can to love it well and show it well to the world is one way you transform nothing into something.

Camus, who delved deep into the Valley of Death, wrote that two or three of those images would give enough meaning to life that you could refuse suicide.

We live in a culture that likely will kill itself through resource exhaustion or total war or overbreeding. Perhaps that in itself is enough justification to believe in nothing. Certainly it's cause to be deeply skeptical of those things the culture tells us are life-giving. Certainly it gives heft to the belief that we are in for a long winter of the soul. Certainly you can say that Santa Claus won't brighten that winter to a noticeable degree.

BUT AT ONE POINT in his life Ezra Pound had to have intuited that in the image was a doorway to a different and better
world. Pound lost that fine intuition and became imprisoned in
this world in many more ways than one.

Robert Bly's poem "A Home in Dark Grass" contains an
image that stands in soulful counterpoint to Pound's much-
quoted line, "what thou lovest well remains":

> We did not come to remain whole.
> We came to lose our leaves like the trees
> The trees that are broken
> And start again, drawing up from the great roots.

There's an imperative for you.

Rules for Writers

Ezra Pound's Ten Tips for Dealing with the Shadows in the Blank Screen

1. If an image sticks in your mind, it will generate a story or poem if you let it.

2. If a story or poem isn't ending well, go back to the point where you saw what you had to do next and decided it was too scary or too much work, and took the easy way out.

3. The blank screen isn't a metaphor for your soul until you put a sentence or two down. Then it's a metaphor for your soul under construction. Write a paragraph, a chapter, a book on that screen—there's the start of a soul there, however small, however humble.

4. Don't ignore your dreams. Especially don't ignore the dream images that stay with you when you're awake and wandering around in your underwear, looking for a cup of coffee.

5. The night-sea journey or the Valley of Death will have its moment in everything you write. It will feel like nothing is working, nothing will ever work, and no matter what success you've had up until now, you'll never write again. That's the moment when stories and poems get forged, the moment when you most need to drive yourself forward.

6. Dream as a god, write as a mortal. They're not called deadlines for nothing.

7. An image will contain imperatives. Don't ignore them, especially if one of those imperatives is to write something.

8. A *ménage a trois* will not improve your mood. Neither will old age. Put them together, and they both become worse and can mess up your writing.

9. Don't write stuff that you know you will succeed at. It will destroy your belief in Mr. Dumb Luck, your writing partner.

10. Just because Ezra Pound got caught up in evil, it doesn't mean you have to reject the whole of his life. Separate the bad from the good, and keep the good. They're not that hard to tell apart.

4

Writing Family

What do we love so much we want to protect it from strangers?
—Robert Bly

EACH OF US bears a family on our shoulders whether we want to or not. So there are children, brothers or sisters, mothers or fathers, grandparents or great grandparents reading this chapter along with you. When you sit down to write, they'll be right there too.

Your family has the ability to travel with you even when all you've bought is a ticket for one. When you look at other people, you don't see family faces right away. But as you begin to feel part of a group, and that group has an identity, the faces of strangers suddenly begin to seem familiar.

Familiar. Family-ar.

A STORY you've written comes before a writing workshop and one of the other workshop members—up to right now your newest best friend—speaks that deadly phrase, "I liked it, but..." and then he says something awful about your story, the story you poured your heart and soul into, the story that you finally found the courage to tell.

Suddenly you can't hear anything at all. Your ears stop functioning. However, your vision gets better. You can see what you hadn't before: that's not your best friend, that's your *sibling* sitting here in the workshop with you.

You look to the workshop instructor, but she seems to be paying serious attention to what your sibling is saying, and there's a rule that you can't say anything about your story while it's being workshopped because your writing is supposed to speak for itself, and it *would,* except this—this *person,* this former newest best friend—hasn't even *read* your story.

Now he's saying the same thing about your story that the instructor said about a story last week, and the instructor is nodding and smiling like he's saying something smart. Can't she see what he's doing? No, she can't, obviously. How'd she get to be a workshop instructor anyway? Spilled her guts over a ream of paper and called it a memoir. Put a bunch of depressing midnight diary entries into a book and called it poetry. And even if she could write, she can't teach.

Two can play this game. Your ex-newest-best-friend's story is up tomorrow. He didn't read yours but you're going to read his. You're going to read it line by line, and write detailed notes in tiny handwriting in the margins, and when he gets it back he's going to know something about you that he didn't know before: that you value honesty, even if it hurts.

It's the only way to help him improve as a writer.

I CONDUCTED my first creative writing workshop in September of 1974. It was full of ninth and tenth graders in a small private school in Sun Valley, Idaho. The author of my first workshopped story left the room in tears. I felt terrible. Then the author of my second workshopped story left the room in tears. When the third story came up I asked the person in the workshop who had been doing most of the talking to shut up. I didn't realize it at the time, but she had brought her invisible but incisive and critical mother into my workshop. When I told her to shut up, the mother vanished completely and the daughter—suddenly alone and facing a bunch of angry people—left the room in tears.

In the thirty years since that time I've learned less about running a workshop than you might think, but I do intervene a little more quickly and gently when workshop dynamics seem to be leading to tears.

It's an inexact science. There's something about sitting around a table with stories in our hands that brings up our family dinners, dinners where the leftover pot roast isn't the only evidence of carnage when the table is ready for clearing.

James Hillman, in his essay, "Extending the Family" writes: "The sign 'Home Cooking' might still bring in some customers, but for many the family table [is] the place of trauma…Here, at the table, family fights over money, politics or morals are most likely to break out, and… [the very notion of what constitutes 'good' food takes on its definitive form.] Here anorexia and bulimia—[and obesity]—appear first. Whether the atmosphere at meals is boisterous and competitive, or chaotic, or gravely formalized, tension is always on the menu."

Without much effort, you can probably remember the worst

family dinner you ever attended, what made it so awful, and why you get angry every time you think about it. Sitting at a table with a story in your hands isn't so different from sitting at a table with bread in your hands, and a glass of wine in front of you, and a secret nobody wants to talk about on everybody's mind.

THERE'S A REASON that I'm addressing you in the Second Person Aggressive. When someone starts talking about family or stories, it's all too easy to imagine that it's not your family and not your story that's being talked about.

But, yes, I'm talking about *your* family, the one you grew up in, the people that you carry with you as you read this. And I'm talking about your story, which may be yours alone or—more likely—may be the one your family forced upon you.

I am also addressing you as a writer, and no family is indifferent to having a writer in its midst. They are with you to make sure that you get an education, but that you don't learn anything they don't want you to learn, or write anything they don't want you to write.

One way to define a family is that it's a secret-keeping machine, and writers are the finders and blabbers of secrets.

One of the things MFA stands for is Might Freely Admit. And what you might freely admit is that Uncle Ernie lives down in the crawl space and seems to be quite happy there, at least since the operation. Or that Cousin Elmer, the fire-and-brimstone preacher, is being hounded for money by that girl he got pregnant when he was in high school. Or little Johnny can't have a pet because the last three rabbits he got for his birthdays died in horrible ways.

THE FAMILY'S FEAR is that you might freely admit the truth, and it doesn't have to be a truth that anyone else would see as damaging to the family. My original title for this chapter, "If You Publish That, You'll Kill Your Mother," is a quote from my brother, who had just read the manuscript for *Traplines*, my memoir. At the time, it had been accepted for publication by Pantheon, and my reaction to his warning was, "Well, I guess she's gonna die."

What he was talking about was a passage I had written about my father's death that described how painful his last month was. What my mother said upon reading that passage was, "Thank you for that wonderful tribute to your father's courage." It didn't kill her at all.

What I've figured out since my brother told me not to publish is that *he's* terribly frightened of dying alone in a hospital at 3 A.M. I'm afraid of that, too, but I've admitted it could happen and therefore can write about it. My brother doesn't want to admit that, and I'm not so sure that his isn't the right approach. He doesn't wake up at 3 A.M. and think about dying, like I do, or if he does he doesn't tell me.

What my brother read in my manuscript for *Traplines* wasn't there. It was potentially there, and terrifying thoughts were sparked into being when he read the manuscript.

That's one reason your family might not want you to publish your memories of your adolescent years. Publication gives a cultural heft to your story. It's hard to ignore a published writer, and even harder to ignore the stories that writer tells. You can write miserable self-obsessed poetry and hide it in the bottom left-hand drawer of your dresser, and your family may call you a poet. But publish one of those miserable self-obsessed poems in *The New Yorker*, and in response to the congratulations of family friends and old high-school teachers, a father is likely to say, "I don't know where she learned that stuff. Certainly not from me." But chances are you did learn some misery or self-obsession from him. If you turned that misery and self-obsession into publishable poetry, good for you. Your father isn't going to like what you did with his gifts.

In my time in the classroom I have learned that if you stand at the lectern and shoot your mouth off about anorexia, or incest, or bankruptcy, or someone who sits at home and watches TV all day and won't get a job, or a child given up for adoption, you will stab two or three people right in the heart. Unless they're writers. Then you give them an idea for a story.

JOAN DIDION ends her preface to *Slouching Towards Bethlehem* with the sentence, "That is one thing to remember: *writers are always selling somebody out.*" Kurt Vonnegut had a riff he repeated to his college audiences who showed up for an evening of being lectured to by someone who actually made money being a writer. He told them, "I realize that some of you may have come in hopes of hearing tips on how to become a professional writer. I say to you, 'If you really want to hurt your parents, and you don't have the nerve to be a homosexual, the least you can do is go into the arts.'"

Vonnegut is being funny here by twisting an unfunny truth, which is that if you're homosexual, it's likely that you know far more about the power of family than if you're heterosexual. Even if parents aren't worried, siblings are. And if siblings aren't, aunts or uncles or children are. In almost every instance the worry for them is going to be a lot less if you stay in the closet. Families are conservative institutions, which is why political and social conservatives constantly invoke them, even when their policies starve children and destroy educational institutions and ostracize some members of families.

But Vonnegut isn't really talking about homosexuality. He is talking about writing, and how it can be seen as something shameful yet powerful and seductive by people who stand on the outside of it. Vonnegut could have put it differently. He could have said, "If you want to really find out if your family loves you or hates you, become a writer."

IN *THE POLITICS OF EXPERIENCE,* R.D. Laing discusses how our experience—that thing we get from living in the world—is modified and sometimes destroyed by violence masquerading as love. The book portrays culture in violent conflict with the individual, and contains this sentence, written in 1964: "In the past fifty years, we human beings have slaughtered by our own hands...one hundred million of our own species. We all live under the threat of total annihilation...we are driven to kill and be killed as we are to live and let live. Only by the most outrageous violation of ourselves [can we] adjust to a civilization driven to its own destruction."

I like *The Politics of Experience* because it gives me permission to think the unthinkable: civilization is insane and if I don't separate myself from it and get some perspective on its ongoing self-destruction, I will be insane, too.

Laing is explicit: "From the moment of birth...the baby is

subjected to these forces of violence, called love, as its mother and father, and their parents and their parents before them, have been. These forces are mainly concerned with destroying most of its potentialities, and on the whole this enterprise is successful. By the time the new human being is fifteen or so, we are left with a being like ourselves, a half-crazed creature more or less adjusted to a mad world. This is normality in our present age."

I loved this stuff forty years ago. It gave psychiatric sanction to what I was intuiting at a time when our government was in the act of destroying another nation for its own profit. It told me to be sane in an insane world, and in that command I found a great freedom.

So I did not have to die in Vietnam. I did not have to enter the harness of matrimony or the prison of morality. I could ingest illegal substances if I felt like it, and have sex with people I'd only known for a few hours. I didn't have to have a house in the suburbs or a career. I didn't have to make more money than a bare minimum, because money was an express ticket to madness.

I love this stuff now, too, but I've learned that total freedom, if I might be permitted a rock concert metaphor, starts out at Woodstock and ends, sickeningly soon, at the Altamont Raceway. The equivalent literary metaphor is that we should read Thomas Hobbes's *Leviathan*, with its bleak view of human nature, along with *The Politics of Experience*.

Laing himself wrote a book called *The Politics of the Family* a few years later, and if *The Politics of Experience* is like a jailbreak for the mind, *The Politics of the Family* is like a week after that jailbreak, when you're hiding in a culvert, wet and cold, listening to the hounds bay. Because Laing stopped saying that there was a way out. Instead, he started analyzing the family that we all have inside of us, and how it got there, and the near-total impossibility of doing anything about it.

When Laing writes about your family being with you, he's referring to a set of people who might have once been on your outside but who have since made places for themselves on your inside. If you close your eyes, you can probably see your mother's face. She's sitting there with you, inside you.

It's a switch to have your mother inside of you.

But Laing's concept of family includes not just interior people but also "an interior set of relations." In other words, beyond the images of your family that you carry inside you, you also carry a deep understanding of how people work when they're in a group.

It's much harder to escape the way-people-work concept than it is to reject a family religion or family definitions of gender or a position in the family corporation or a tradition of family military service.

Laing says structures of the family become the structures of our mind. The experience of the family becomes our own experience. The dreams of the family become the landscapes of our sleep.

THESE DAYS Laing has lost his luster as a psychotherapist, partly because of advances in neurochemistry, but also because his message was one of paranoia: a diagnosis of mental illness is often the result of seeing things as they are instead of believing in the lies of our family or our culture. He may be right—I think he is right, at least for writers—but a belief that you're right and the rest of the world is wrong is not a step on the road to peace of mind.

Research into the brain chemistry of schizophrenics has provided more acceptable metaphors for what is going on when you go crazy. But there are a few defenders of Laing who point out that to see through the fictions of family and culture is such a powerful and alienating experience in itself that it can alter your brain chemistry.

In any event, I find Laing a very good psychologist for writers, one who is not so reductive that he transforms our art into a pile of dead components. Instead, he offers a way to disobey family orders, and shows you the metaphorical machine guns those family orders were telling you to charge into.

He also offers a way to tell the truth through telling stories. He suggests that stories are things that we are born into, live in, and die out of. It's hard to see them from the outside. But if you can look at your family story from the outside, you've passed a milepost on the road to becoming a writer. An alienated writer. An estranged writer. But a writer.

LET'S LEAVE Laing for a while. Let me tell you a story.

In the fall of 1964, I fell in love. I was fourteen and a brand-new high school student. I was in the midst of setting a school record for geekiness, but that didn't stop me from becoming infatuated with Cassandra Greene, the homecoming queen that year. Cassandra was small-boned and delicate and sprite-like, with great dark eyes and a mass of tumbling black hair that reached her waist. She was, to my unpracticed eyes, the most beautiful woman in the high school and maybe the world. She was seventeen and a senior.

There were fewer than two hundred students in our high

school and I would see Cassandra in the hallways almost every day. To my amazement, she liked me. She would call me by name, a kindness seniors almost never gave to freshmen. She smiled at me. She asked me how my classes were going.

It took a week for me to develop a monster crush on her, which lasted until I asked her if I could walk her home from school. She told me no. She only lived about a block from the school and there wasn't any point in it.

Not long after, I saw her laughing with one of her girlfriends. I decided that they were laughing at me, a freshman boy, thinking he could walk a senior woman home from school. The rest of the week was horrible. I avoided her until the homecoming football game, when I stood with the rest of the crowd at halftime and watched the captain of the football team place a tiara on her head and a kiss on her lips. It was the bitterest moment of my young life.

Then Cassandra burst into tears and began sobbing. She smiled through the sobs and everyone cheered and then the ceremony was over. The game started and even though I don't remember if we won, I still remember her smiling face, streaked with tears, across forty-six years.

But her smile wasn't a smile. When I looked at it recently in my high school yearbook, I found Cassandra's homecoming queen picture. Her smile was what romance writers call a rictus of pain, and above what I had thought a smile were two sad eyes.

Over the years, I've learned that you can cry when you're happy and smile when you're not. I also learned within my first year in high school that you can get over a painful romantic crush, especially if you get another crush on someone else. I started dating—not successfully, but dating. I forgot Cassandra and didn't go to her graduation, and haven't seen her in person since.

But she has remembered me her entire life. That sounds like a vain and self-obsessed thing to say, but it's true. I found that out twenty years later, when I was in a hotel in San Francisco, waiting to get on a plane to Bangkok. With me was Blake, a teaching colleague and friend who happened to be Cassandra's nephew—though I didn't know that.

Blake and I were both on sabbatical, and single. We had money in savings and were looking forward to three months traveling around Southeast Asia. It was a moment where if you had asked me if I had a care or obligation or worry in the world, I would have said no.

We had a day before our plane left, and Blake said he wanted to visit his uncle, who worked in one of the cities across the Bay. He told me his uncle's name, and I said I knew the guy from high school. Blake then told me his uncle was married to Cassandra Greene. It was a moment of wonderful coincidence, or at least I thought so at the time. Blake phoned his uncle to find out how to get to their house.

Everything went fine until Blake asked, "Is it okay if I bring John Rember with me?" There was a silence, and then Blake's uncle asked if he could call him back. Five minutes later the phone rang. His uncle said it was a bad time to visit and we should go to Thailand and see them some other time.

So we went out for beer and Blake told me a story about his uncle and his Aunt Cassandra. They had begun dating in high school, and sometime in the spring of her sophomore year Cassandra had gotten pregnant. Cassandra's father had imprisoned her in their home while he held a series of secret meetings with Blake's grandfather to decide what to do. Blake said the two men would meet at night in one of the canyons outside of town, with a prearranged signal: three headlight flashes, followed by a single flash. That was so they could recognize each other out there among the deer and the sagebrush and any other patriarchs trying to decide the fate of pregnant high school sophomores.

The two fathers decided that Cassandra and Blake's uncle would be separated. Cassandra would go to a home for unwed mothers, have the child, and give it up for adoption. Blake's uncle, away at college, would be forbidden to see Cassandra ever again.

Cassandra disappeared from school her junior year, reappeared her senior year, and was elected homecoming queen by the Lettermen's Club, which is the way our high school selected its homecoming royalty. Her baby had been a girl. She had given her up for adoption. The child, for all most people in the high school knew, never existed.

Two years later, Cassandra and Blake's uncle ran away and got married. When Cassandra's father died a decade later, they were still estranged from him. The old man had forbidden Cassandra's mother to be in touch with Cassandra or even speak of her. When he died, Cassandra's mother was finally able to see her own daughter again.

IN THE MIDDLE of my crush on Cassandra, I had wondered why she didn't have a boyfriend. That question was soon replaced by: if she didn't have a boyfriend, why not me? I had known nothing about how Cassandra had spent her junior year, but she assumed that I knew everything about her history.

Sometimes you not only don't know the answer, you don't know enough to not ask the question, and you don't even know the question not to ask.

But sitting in a bar in San Francisco in 1984, I was able to understand how a smile could be a rictus of pain, and how it was not good to be queen at Wood River High School in 1964, which is why Blake and I couldn't show up at her door. Her father and her father-in-law would have been with us.

A YEAR AGO Blake told me there was more to this story. Cassandra and Blake's uncle had had four children after they were married. They had kept the secret of the sister they had given away from the rest of their kids. By the time all four children had reached college age, Cassandra and Blake's uncle were finding their lives to be long on misery. They had decided to get divorced.

They were in the middle of the divorce when their long-lost daughter showed up on their doorstep. She had been able to track them down because of changes in confidentiality policy regarding adoptions. She was thirty-six years old, and an attorney.

I'd like to be able to tell you that she did their divorce for them, but instead her appearance was taken as a divine command for a complete and utter reconciliation. God spoke, in the language of grandfathers.

SO WHERE do you suppose individual free will fits in Cassandra's story? Where do family secrets, family taboos, family traditions, and angry patriarchs leave off and where does Cassandra's life begin? What do Cassandra's four, now five, children think of their grandfathers? What must it have been like to grow up with a shadow sibling? Were they aware of a ghost on Christmas morning? Was there a shadow under the tree? Was there a gift still hidden in the top of the hall closet?

LET US GO BACK to R.D. Laing for help with this story. Laing provides some useful ways of looking at the family rules that make a story like Cassandra's possible. He starts at a basic level, writing that, "…by [the time you're one year old] the following distinctions have come to be made:"

- inside and outside
- pleasure and pain
- real and not real
- good and bad
- me and not me
- here and there
- then and now

You probably didn't come to these distinctions by trial and error in your first year. Your family made them for you. If you had made them for yourself, all hell would have broken loose, as it must have when you put something icky inside your mouth that was supposed to remain on your outside.

Laing has a simple thought experiment that shows how powerfully we make these distinctions:

1. Swallow the saliva in your mouth.
2. Take a glass of water, sip from it and swallow.
3. Spit in the glass of water, swallow spit and water.
4. Sip from the glass of water, spit it back, sip again and swallow.

Laing is demonstrating that essentially the same operation—the swallowing of saliva—becomes four different things when you play with the barrier between inside and outside, me and not me, here and there, and so on. Imagine those same distinctions coming into play if you're a small-town Idaho businessman who has just discovered that his fifteen-year-old is pregnant. Imagine those distinctions coming into play if Cassandra, instead of eloping at nineteen, had gone to her father and told him she was going to become a writer, and she's going to write about giving away her child.

It's likely that Cassandra would see her book as now-here-me-good-real-painful-inside, while her father would have seen the book as then-there-not me-bad-unreal-painful-outside. The only thing they would agree on is the pain.

"It didn't happen that way. What you think happened to you was not real," is just one of the lies he would have told her, and she wouldn't have written the book. If her shame kept her story from her four other children for thirty years, could she have put it into words on paper?

I tell my students that on the page it's safe to do all the things you want to do but wouldn't dare to in the physical world, but on the level of family taboo, putting it into words and publishing it is far worse than doing it.

Here are some things that families have said to my writing students:

- Why don't you get a degree in something that will make you money?
- Written that best-seller yet?
- Why do you want to dredge that up again?

- Those are all lies. We didn't send you to college to learn to tell lies.
- I didn't like your novel, but I really liked that garden article you did for *Sunset Magazine.*
- Don't most writers drink too much?
- You are so talented. You could do a lot of other things.
- It's so good to have a writer in the family. Grandfather's story needs to be told.

LAING SAYS it's easier to see how dysfunctional families work than it is to see how functional families work. He suggests that the rules may be stronger and subtler in functioning families, and the freedom less, the hope for change nonexistent.

Writing is one of the rare professions where a dysfunctional family can help your career. Because if the family rules are irrational, or crazy, or unjust, there's a chance that you might see them as arbitrary and breakable rules, and one of the jobs of a writer—to paraphrase my colleague, the poet Marvin Bell—is to find the rules and break the rules. If the rules are working perfectly and you're feeling free within their invisible lines, it's much harder to find them.

HERE'S WHAT a few other writers have done with family dysfunction:

In her novel *Other Women,* the writer Lisa Alther tells the story of a competent, intelligent psychotherapist who goes to her parents' home for Thanksgiving. Within a few hours of crossing her parents' threshold, she is reduced to a crying, screaming adolescent, as unable to function as the most neurotic of her clients.

Her sophisticated education and wisdom are gone. The rages she felt as a teenager with a curfew are back.

In John Cheever's short story "Goodbye, My Brother," the narrator, a kindly and articulate English teacher—all English teachers are kindly and articulate—who loves sailing and dancing and beautiful women and the conviviality that comes with alcohol, is confronted by his little brother, who loves none of those things, and ends up beating him over the head with a piece of driftwood as they walk upon the beach.

In Faulkner's *The Sound and the Fury*, Benjy, the only character free from the dictates of Southern culture and Southern family, is castrated because he can't be controlled by family standards of decency.

In Tennessee Williams' play *Suddenly Last Summer*, a young woman who exposes her brother's homosexuality is sedated while her mother tells her doctors to lobotomize her: "Cut that lie out of her," is the old woman's way of putting it.

Eugene O'Neill wrote *Long Day's Journey into Night* to lay the tormented dead of his family to rest, and in doing so guaranteed their tormented immortality.

In Harold Pinter's *The Homecoming*, a father and older brother conspire to have sex with a younger brother's new wife, home to meet the family.

And then there's memoir. Every memoir, including my own, is a detailed explanation of how people act in a group, told by someone who doesn't quite want to believe what he's saying.

SOMETHING GOOD comes out of all of this: once you have the courage to look at the secrets your secret-keeping machine is keeping, you can gain tremendous energy for writing. I'm oversimplifying, but Laing defines the operation of repression as deliberately forgetting what little Johnny did to his pet rabbits, deliberately forgetting that there were rabbits, forgetting that you've forgotten what little Johnny did, and forgetting what you've forgotten he did it to. Depending on what little Johnny did to the rabbits in the first place, these forgetting-that-you've-forgotten operations can have layers upon layers. They're invisible, but their presence is discernable in a manner similar to the way astronomers discern the presence of black holes. There's a distinct borderline where enormous amounts of energy disappear.

One job for the writer in your family is to release that secret-keeping energy so parents, siblings, grandparents, aunts and uncles can use it to escape from their cells in the family prison. But only if they want to.

The job is dangerous and frightening because we look at the family for our final survival—probably as a result of a million years or so of bad children being tossed out into the darkness beyond the campfire. We can't just reject our families, no matter how much they have hurt us, no matter if, as Laing says, "The family's function is to repress Eros; to induce a false consciousness of security; to deny death by avoiding life; to cut off transcendence; to believe in God, not to experience the Void; to create in short, one dimensional [humans]."

Even with all the semicolons, most people will choose to belong to a family and lose all but the most boring dimensions of themselves rather than face the loss of the family campfire.

Writers who face that blank screen know what it's like to be kicked out of the family circle. It's lonely. It's cold. It's dangerous.

But it's a place of freedom, and if you're lucky, you can use that freedom to tell a secret. When you tell that secret, you get back a little bit of power, and with that power—it's the power to tell the simple truth—you can tell another secret and gain more power and that power can result in poems and plays and novels and memoirs and sometimes in angry letters and even suicide notes if the poems and plays and novels and memoirs don't work out. It's a dangerous business that writers choose to be in.

One way of looking at your task as a writer is to drag your family kicking and screaming into your experience, rather than having them provide your experience for you and tell you what it means. When you look at it this way, and look at the other things I've told you in this chapter, it's possible to conclude that the writer and the writer's family are natural enemies. That's right. But as in other instances of Mutually Assured Destruction, peace, cooperation, and even the exchange of ambassadors are possible.

YOU HAD NO CHOICE about what your family inscribed upon you when you were two or three. But if you're a writer, you have the ability to write down those inscriptions and think about them and play with them. In doing so, it's possible to examine which parts of you are truly your own and which parts still belong to your family. Over time, you can increase the proportion of what is your own. Striking a blow for human freedom begins in your own heart, with your own blank screen, doing your own sorting between you and not you, and finding out what you brought to the table, and what was brought to the table for you.

Rules for Writers

Ten Fun Family Facts for Writers

1. Families are secret-keeping machines.

2. Families don't like trouble-makers. Writers tell family secrets. Therefore, writers are trouble-makers.

3. Every family has a hastily invented alibi for being the way it is, one that's full of holes if you look closely at it.

4. Usually you can write things you wouldn't dare do. But in families, you can do things you wouldn't dare write.

5. A family will fight to stay true to its idea of itself, even at the expense of the people in it.

6. Writing will put you outside of the family, looking in. But it'll only *feel* like you're going to die.

7. Your family has taught you how people behave in a group.

8. American League Baseball teams have designated hitters. Families have designated crazy people. As a writer, you won't even have to raise your hand.

9. Families don't read books. You will not get to listen to a discussion of your book during Thanksgiving Dinner, unless you've written a book on turkeys. Don't write a book on turkeys.

10. Your family, no matter how full of pathology, is a gift to your art.

5

Writing Place

And forgive us our trespasses, as we forgive them that trespass against us.

—The Book of Common Prayer

LONG AGO, when I was contemplating what to do in life, I didn't decide to become a writer. I decided to become a ski instructor. I had grown up in Sun Valley, Idaho, and had seen the ski instructors there enjoy themselves. Many of them had married attractive older women who had come to Sun Valley in the midst of divorces from doctors, lawyers, and CEOs. These women had signed up for private ski lessons while they waited for court dates, and their lessons led to après-ski drinks with their instructors, the drinks led to dinners, and so on.

The instructors, upon marriage, became wealthy. They bought Porsches, took flying lessons, paid off the bar tabs of old enemies, and flirted with waitresses during long alcoholic lunches in Sun Valley's restaurants after skiing a couple of hours in the mornings.

Not a bad route to old age, I decided. But when I told my plan to my father, he said, "Son, don't do anything for money that you like to do for fun."

He had been a fishing guide in Sawtooth Valley for twenty summers, and he was afraid my plans to spend life skiing would end up like his plans to spend life fishing. He didn't remember the fish he had caught nearly as well as he remembered the long string of mediocre fishermen to whom he had handed fish on the line. I suspect he thought that my joy in skiing would disappear in the middle of guiding lowing herds of novice skiers down an endless beginner's slope. After he stopped guiding, it was a long time before my father threw a hook in the water again.

My father's words came back to me several summers ago. I had walked out of my house and across the pasture to my sauna. It's a heavy-duty industrial sauna, an eight-by-ten frame shack with four inches of Styrofoam in the walls and ceiling, and a big barrel stove for heat. It sits on the edge of the Salmon River, and it's a nice place to steam yourself silly over an afternoon. When you can't stand the heat any longer, you can jump in the river and float around in a big deep hole until you're nicely chilled, and then head inside to warmth that feels good once again.

I was carrying beer, a mystery novel by James Ellroy called *The Black Dahlia*, a boombox, an armload of wood from the woodpile, and an old pair of running shoes from my garbage can. I had found the shoes in the bottom of a closet a week before, and they were torn, worn, and smelled like Darth Vader might have smelled if he'd been a mushroom. I'd picked them out of the garbage because they were petroleum-based and I thought they'd help start a fire. I threw them into the sauna's stove, threw the wood on top of them, and put a match to them. They started smoking and spitting blue fire. I closed the stove, punched an old Led Zeppelin tape into the boombox, cracked a beer, got naked, opened the book, and sat in sunshine in the open doorway of the sauna, waiting for wood to catch.

It was one of those moments, when—if you could wire your brain up to a recording device that could then replay your entire sensorium to a theater audience—you could sell a small experience for big money. This, in spite of the fact that *The Black Dahlia* is a dark and violent novel, about love and the bitter residue of love betrayed and death and blood and people who never cared enough to raise their kids right. It's set in Los Angeles, but that's not the place to read it. Far better to read it in a small warm shack on the side of a clear-running river in the middle of Idaho, where you don't have to worry that any of it ever could happen to you.

But then I heard something awful. Just upriver from the sauna, on the other side of the fenceline, somebody was cursing. I live next to a Sportsman's Access on the river, and the Idaho Fish and Game Department dumps in thousands of domesticated rainbow trout above my fence during the summer. They're fish that don't have any idea of how to eat in the wild. They'll strike at any fly that looks remotely like a hatchery food pellet.

There were two people waving fly rods on the other side of the fence, a man and a woman, hatted and wadered and creeled and vested. A thick stream of stinking black smoke was coming out of the stovepipe and swirling around them and their fly rods and over the clear water of the Salmon River. I recognized the man as a fishing guide from Sun Valley who took clients to the Sportsman's Access every time a fish truck stopped there.

They thought I had deliberately poisoned the air to run them out of my backyard. But my guests were welcome to all the fish they could get. I was simply trying to keep a pair of fungus-laden running shoes from contaminating a landfill while getting a fire started.

Soon enough the stovepipe started emitting clean woodsmoke. I closed the door, and began reading about an honest and upright policeman falling in love with evil in the form of beauty. I felt the beginnings of a comfortable sweat. But I was not as happy as I had been.

I peeked out at the guide and client, who had crossed the fenceline and were headed down the riverbank in front of me. They had frowns on their faces, frowns that indicated they knew about the riverbank easement the government holds on our property that gave them the right to be there. They were the frowns of ownership.

Then I realized that where the fly-fishing guide and his client stood, my father had stood with *his* clients, fishing for salmon. The woman was paying hundreds of dollars for her opportunity to catch hatchery fish. My father had charged ten dollars a day, and had guaranteed a chinook salmon on the line.

It was impossible at that moment not to feel as though the great had been transformed into the grotesque in the forty years between one transaction and the other. The dams that had stopped the salmon runs had also transformed the Salmon River into a place where farmed fish were released and caught and released and caught until they died.

That was when I remembered my father's advice. I was glad I hadn't become a ski instructor or a fishing guide. They are occupations that trivialize our interactions with the natural world.

I sat in the thick heat of the sauna, looking out its window at the guide and client as they made beautiful casts over the water. They caught a couple of rainbow. Finally they moved downriver and out of sight. I rushed across the gravel bank to the river's edge, dove deep into the hole, and came up gasping and cold.

YOU MAY BE wondering what dark urban crime novels have to do with bright and hopeful river valleys in the American West.

One thing I don't think you're wondering is whether or not a landscape can contain hope. The writer Wallace Stegner coined the phrase "the geography of hope" to describe the American West. But if the West is a landscape of hope, the hope it has represented is hope of a return to Eden, where, in the incarnation that caught Stegner's imagination, the mountains are made of rock candy, and the handouts grow on bushes, the springs are lemonade, and little streams of alcohol come trickling down the rocks.

Toward the end of his life Wallace Stegner wrote that the West wasn't any longer a landscape of hope for him. He had realized that Eden would never be found here, because the idea of Eden could, in and of itself, destroy hope.

Stegner said he had hoped that the West "would someday have a civilization to match its scenery." But the dreams of irrigators, housing developers and real-estate salesmen, resort owners, Bureau of Reclamation engineers, and even those of us who have a little place of our own in the country are far more concerned with transforming the scenery to fit our flawed civilization rather than paying attention to the scenery and then crafting a civilization to fit it.

FINDING EDEN isn't about paying attention to anything outside. It's a yearning to get back *inside* the life of a pampered infant. You will have noticed that my dream of becoming a Sun Valley ski instructor and marrying a wealthy divorcee would be a lot like a return to infancy. So would be a life of fly fishing, for that matter, or living in the country and building a sauna next to water there and spending long afternoons reading trashy novels and listening to classic rock and roll music on an antique boombox. But our geography has aged, even if our yearnings haven't. None of our Edens has been immune to industrial tourism or lowering water tables or population growth or the planting of vast subdivisions on our dwindling supply of fertile farmland.

I'VE GOT a few loose ends here. I'll try to tie up the easy ones first.

First, what happened to the *female* ski instructors? No problem. They found recently divorced doctors and lawyers and CEOs, most of them male, and married them. It leads to a suspicion that ski instructors belong to a mildly parasitic species, one a lot like barnacles but more athletic.

Second, did I end up doing something for money that I used to do for fun? Not really. I became a travel writer and a teacher, each of which has its moments of fun, but never in the midst of a stack of first-semester essays or ten hours into a twenty-hour plane ride.

Third, Ellroy's *The Black Dahlia*, although a fine example of its genre, is not ultimately entertaining even on the banks of the Salmon River. Its vision is so dark that eventually it transforms the bright sunshine, the high wild call of birds, the roar of the rapids, and the smell of summer grasses into something bleak and dangerous. You can put a wall of mountains between L.A. and yourself, but every human heart has its own bleak city, full of shadows, illicit lust, and psychopathic killers.

THOSE ARE the easy loose ends. There are more difficult ones, such as the uncomfortable relationship between humans and the natural world. Ernest Becker, in his grimly ironic work *The Denial of Death*, suggests that humans are gods with their feet stuck fast in their own excrement, beings of unlimited imagination constantly confronted with the inescapable stench of their animal selves.

That's not a loose end easily tied up. But earlier civilizations in the American West used animals as bridges between nature and the restless human spirit. That an animal could serve as a bridge seems improbable until I call it a totem, a magical thing that allows us entry to a different world, one where our imaginations and our bodies can exist in harmony.

Some examples:

- A man will occupy a cubicle and pound a keyboard for fifty weeks and spend money he doesn't have on a rifle, camouflage clothing, a pickup, horses, and a trailer just so he can kill an old bull elk. This ritual will allow him to briefly escape his dental plan, his corroded 401(k), his mortgage, his Visa bill, and his worries about his kids' tuitions.
- A woman, seeing wolf puppies for the first time, will quit her job, move to the mountains, and volunteer to follow a pack of wolves during the best years of her life, seeing in them trusting relationships, a simple and

happy relationship to food, and a stable family hierarchy, all things she has never found in her relationships with men.

- The Yellowstone tourist who watches through binoculars as a grizzly chases a pack of wolves from their kill is briefly not a tourist. He's a witness. He may have maxed out the credit card to get there, but he is not—for that instant—wondering if this vacation, with the kids crying in the back seat of the minivan and his wife angry and silent, was worth it.

We need animal totems to escape from the self-conscious discontent of civilization, and we need them so badly we will pretend they have magical powers even when we've stripped them of their magic. Hatchery-raised fish and elk and deer that have been regulated as intensely as a herd of Holsteins are what industrial tourism offers as doorways to a world where our imaginations and our bodies can coexist.

The reintroduction of wolves to the West is for many the ultimate attempt to allow humans to experience the natural world. But I've heard wildlife biologists say that wolf reintroduction is not about wildlife management at all.

Instead, they say it's about people management, a sad phrase that illustrates that no matter how close you get to your totem animal, you're still looking at it through human eyes. You might yearn for that transcendent moment when your totem pulls you into a deep natural world but if somebody else's totem animal threatens to eat your totem animal, or if someone shoots your totem animal, you start thinking of lawsuits or angry phone calls to your senator. Our culture is a trap that is difficult to escape.

Wildlife biologists end up poring over legal documents in offices rather than becoming rugged backwoods characters with an uncanny understanding of the natural world.

The wolves reintroduced to the West are the product of human politics. When wolves have killed livestock, they have been identified by the radio-collar signatures of the so-called Judas wolves in their packs, and then entire packs have been shot from aircraft. Plans are perennially proposed to negatively condition wolves with shock collars or with nausea-producing bait planted near cattle and sheep herds. If wildlife biologists wanted to save themselves the expense and brutality of domesticating wolves in this manner, they could just go down to a city pound and rescue a few puppies and *call* them wolves.

It's of course possible that we could get rid of livestock on the public lands of the West. Often enough the people who advocate the end of public grazing rights speak of ranchers in the same way Stalin spoke of the kulaks, or Hitler spoke of the Jews—as lice on the body politic. If they were passable students of history, they would realize how ugly their words are. We're not all that far away in time from our own American genocide. Saying that any group needs to be gotten rid of recalls when the people who ran this country saw killing Indians as wildlife management.

At this point, it's a less happy world than it was when I was talking about ski instructing and drinking bottles of wine with lunch and flirting with waitresses making minimum wage and tips. Perhaps in my reading, I should have spent more time with Wallace Stegner and less with James Ellroy. But I want to continue following the thread I'm on, even if it leads to a deep and grieving place in all our hearts, because it shows how good intentions can go bad, and how language designed for truth can become a streamlined vehicle for lies.

Wildlife management becomes management of people. Wildlife science becomes politics. Biologists become biostitutes. Adventure becomes tourism. The animals who were once our wild brothers become walking radio stations or tranquilized, collar-shocked zombies.

What is missing in our dealings with animals is any ability to let them live life on their own terms, in their own world. They cease to have any power to connect us to their world, as we drag them doped or domesticated or dead into ours.

Other civilizations have not made such a hash of things. The Clovis people who lived in the American West a hundred centuries ago were hunters of supreme skill, who created the perfect obsidian, agate, or crystal sculptures we know them by. They mounted those sculptures on shafts and drove them into supercharismatic megafauna—giant bison and woolly mammoths—that after two millennia became extinct.

The Clovis people became extinct, too. After the last of the giant bison and the last of the woolly mammoths, the Clovis points disappear from the archeological record and are replaced by what appear to be the crude hackings of people starting a technology from scratch. Some theorists suggest that the Clovis were hit by an asteroid. I think they collapsed as a civilization when they killed off their totems.

It's tempting to think that if the Clovis had just become vegetarians and sensitive wildlife biologists, we could have mammoths and giant sloths with us now, corralled in Yellowstone with the buffalo and elk and wolves and tourists.

Such thinking ignores the relationship of the Clovis to the

animals they hunted. The animals gave them access to a sacred and sustaining world. It's hard to have a civilization in the absence of such a world.

Before you assume the Clovis quickly destroyed themselves, remember that they lasted ten times longer than the United States has, and they drove fewer species to extinction in their millennia than we have in our centuries.

I think they walked in a beauty we have lost, and that their world was literally ten times *deeper* than ours. It takes generations to develop any understanding of place, and in the American West our civilization has developed in such a way that people are severed from their birthplace every time real estate values allow a profit on their houses. Place becomes the next place or the last place. Our tribal elders cannot distinguish the indigenous from the homogenous, and have less and less need to.

You read, in the footnotes of the history of the West, of bands of Indians begging old cows from ranchers so they could perform ceremonies that once involved buffalo. You read of the ghost dances intended to bring back the buffalo, whose animal magic would push the Europeans back where they came from. The slaughter at Wounded Knee was a response to those dances.

It's easy to see how cultural critics got the idea that Western Civilization contains an imperative to dismember indigenous cultures whenever it discovers them. We're a century and a quarter from Wounded Knee, but we still find that same imperative operating in the American West.

The U.S. Cavalry is no longer killing the locals who insist on staying in their homes. Instead, we use houses whose down payments represent a lifetime of waitressing paychecks. We use property taxes. People management disguised as recreation. People management disguised as real estate investment in mountain communities.

WHEN PEOPLE give up sacred rituals for radio collars, visions of a deeper world for topographic maps of this one, and the magic of animals for ownership over them, they cut off an essential connection to the world. When humans tranquilize an animal, cage it, put a collar on it, domesticate it, and profit from it as a tourist attraction, they've lost access to the beauty and wonder that the animal once offered them.

So. Another loose end. Ski resorts in the West. In 1976 a California developer named Bill Janss owned the Sun Valley Resort and was trying to sell it. He had bought it from Union Pacific and had inherited union contracts with his bus drivers and ski lift mechanics. But Janss had been told that the union needed to be broken before any sale could go through. When the bus drivers' contract expired, no new contract was offered. The drivers and ski lift mechanics went on strike.

The result was a disaster for the community. The national union was not concerned with a strike at a ski resort that was no longer owned by a railroad, and didn't support its local chapter. The strike was broken.

Sun Valley was sold to Earl Holding, a Utah oilman, who didn't rehire those who had been on the picket lines. He hired non-union people willing to work for less money and fewer benefits. Many long-time Sun Valley workers left the area, even when their families had been there for generations.

My father was one of them. He had been a bus driver in the winter at Sun Valley, but years before had bought forty acres in Sawtooth Valley as a base for his guiding business. After the strike, he and my mother moved there. While he spent the rest of his working life on road construction projects, living in a trailer wherever the job was, he always returned to Sawtooth Valley when the jobs ended. He found in his forty acres a place to stand and touch the world without having to destroy it.

Even well-married ski instructors don't have that kind of privilege. Neither did Bill Janss. Late in his life he began to regret selling out to Earl Holding. Janss hadn't needed the money, and had come to the conclusion, helped by a visit to a monastery in Tibet, that humans couldn't really own mountains anyway—humans were just temporary caretakers of sacred places.

Janss began to see that he could have been a better caretaker of Bald Mountain than Earl Holding, who from all appearances didn't believe in any of that Buddhist crap, especially the part about ownership being an illusion. So Bill Janss died needing the sacred more than he needed the money he got for it.

Holding still holds the mountain in his grasp, although that grasp is weakening. Like the rest of us, he's mortal. And when we die we leave behind our money and land and descendants, all of whom are notoriously indifferent to the long-term desires of the once living.

When I think of old Indians completing buffalo rituals using dying cows, I can imagine a sad and final ritual for rich old white men—negotiating for the naming rights of the hospital room they've been brought to. That may be unfair, but hospice people have a saying that we die just as we lived, which means we should consider the impossible juxtaposition of ownership and death before we get too close to either of them.

Impossibility aside, we shouldn't forget that the original meaning of the word *Eden* was walled garden, which suggests that Adam and Eve really didn't get thrown out of it by an angel because they altered their consciousness with an apple. Instead, they quit paying to be in a place that somebody had gone to all the time and expense to put a wall around. They had maxed out their credit cards and it was time for them to go.

Deep within the Garden of Eden myth is the even more powerful myth of ownership. You can have paradise to yourself, or if you wish, you can make people pay to visit it.

Such perceptions underlie more *public* land-use disputes in the West than anyone involved in those disputes would admit. It's at the heart of the debates about wilderness and snowmobile use in Yellowstone Park. When I see and smell the white-blue oilsmoke streaming from a snowmobile as it heads off onto a snow-covered mountain, I realize that mountain is off-limits for me unless I have a snowmobile. You have to breathe too much if you're on skis. Smoke, as I discovered the day I burnt up my running shoes, can act as a wall, complete with Keep Out signs.

But so can a thousand dollars a night for a hotel room. So can a lift ticket that costs a day's wage. So can rising property values that raise taxes beyond the ability of old people to pay. Even a wilderness boundary can act as a wall.

The Garden of Eden comes with exclusionary clauses, and even if you're the owner you spend lots of time and energy keeping those exclusions in place. Eventually you tire and sell out, and become excluded yourself, in the manner of Bill Janss and anyone else who has taken money for a chunk of the sacred. In the end, the only time Eden qualifies as Stegner's landscape of hope is when you're on the outside looking in. Inside, hope turns to the fear that somebody's going to take it away from you, or camp on the lawn without paying.

GUIDING DUDES for a living might not seem like a loose end, but it is. One problem with making a living in the West is that as tourism becomes more and more of our economy, it's getting harder not to be a guide. A good many of the people I know are river guides, horseback guides, kayak guides, hunting guides, backcountry guides, or fly-fishing guides.

The people who ride boats down the Middle Fork of the Salmon, the horseback riders, and the people with new fly rods and waders—they're all paying big money for their experience. They expect their money to guarantee contact with the natural world. If they didn't care about that world, they could stay home and plug into the Internet, or hang out in the Jacuzzi and pretend they're in white water, or rent a video of *A River Runs Through It*, or hop on a merry-go-round pony.

So they go out and hire a guide—a bipedal totem animal. Unfortunately, the guides have been thoroughly domesticated. They've rafted the Middle Fork a hundred times. They've saddled the horses a thousand. They know every bend in the trail, every rapid and every fishing hole. They know that hatchery rainbow aren't real fish.

The guides know that their clients will get a planned and predictable experience unless they wander off the trail, or get bucked into a rock pile full of rattlesnakes, or hit a tree at the edge of the ski run, or drown. Most clients retain attorneys for the unpredictable moments.

As the West has become less dependent on agriculture and mining and more and more on tourism, our states, our back yards, and even our lives become somebody else's vacation. If you're a guide or a ski instructor, where is your experience in somebody else's paid-for experience? Worse yet, what do you do when it's time for *you* to go on vacation? Don't tell me that you'll go somewhere and hire a guide. You shouldn't pay money to have an experience that normally would be yours for the price of walking out into the world and paying attention to it.

I'M DEFINING HOPE by what it isn't. Hope isn't commodifying or standardizing the scenery. Hope isn't our tendency to ignore and even destroy the sacred if it won't fit inside a church. It isn't in our need to own the land rather than caretake it. It isn't even in ecosystems if restoration is yet another excuse to beat up on people and kick them out of their homes. As long as humans are on the planet, any ecosystem will include human sensibility, and it matters whether that sensibility is cruel or kind. In the American West, it's been cruel for centuries.

Not great news. But if you're going to construct a second geography of hope, you shouldn't construct it out of the false promises that led to the collapse of the first one. Think of that honest young cop in *The Black Dahlia*, who ends the novel disillusioned, bitter, and deeply ashamed that his ability to love, his appreciation for beauty, and his pride in his own honor all drew him into an addictive web of evil.

False hope is worse than no hope at all. At least that's what I tell my students, because they need to be able to write about what their civilization is doing before they can write about the land that lies under it. Or be in the world without pushing other people out of it. Or deal with animals in ways that don't involve turning them into personal property or killing and eating them to satisfy poorly understood psychic needs.

I assign my students an essay by Bill Joy, the former chief scientist at Sun Microsystems. It's called "Why the Future Doesn't Need Us." It's a grim prediction that three developing technologies—genetic engineering, nanotechnology, and robotics—might each result in human extinction by 2050. By the end of the essay, Joy, despite his name, has provided a convincing argument that technology unmediated by consciousness will kill us all.

I tell my students that if a plague of self-replicating killer robots destroys us all in 2030, at least one of us will have seen in concert The Doors, Jefferson Airplane, Led Zeppelin, and the Grateful Dead. It's a joke that doesn't get much laughter, because the bands of the 1960s don't have much hold on the imagination of people who can't claim they were at Woodstock, even as embryos.

The 1960s themselves don't inspire my own generation like they used to. Few people are talking about going out into the desert and starting a free-love commune because we've seen how that turns out for the kids. Few people are taking drugs to expand their minds because we've seen more than one consciousness-advocating, flower-toting peace-seeker morph over time into a Ted Kaczynski, going quietly and murderously crazy in a Montana shack.

Joy's essay quotes from Kaczynski's *Unabomber Manifesto,* to show that even paranoid schizophrenics can see that humans are threatened by technology. The *Manifesto* suggests that intelligent machines will win a struggle with humans and that our species will join all the other discontinued models on the scrap heap of evolution.

Joy suggests a more direct route to extinction, which is that the destructive power that can be recorded on a computer disk or grown in a Petri dish or found in a single self-replicating nano-bot will find its way to the next brilliant but unconscious individual who finds murder a way to make his point.

My students aren't comfortable with Joy's ideas, but they need to consider their hopes in the light of his implied questions. In the face of extinction, why get up in the mornings? Why choose between right and wrong, or assume there's any basis for the choice? Why write?

The largest question Joy asks is this: is technology a form of suicide? It's clear that he thinks the answer is yes. I think so, too. I only have to think of Madame Curie, messing about with pitchblende, unaware that her work would begin the process that a half-century later would fry Hiroshima and the people in it.

In the American West—and in western civilization in general—we rest many of our hopes on technology. They are hopes having to do with building sustainable communities centered around computer chip manufacture or telecommuting or bioengineering or software design.

But in a long series of booms and busts, technology may be the biggest bust of all. I've noticed that the people who are still hoping for rock candy mountains and lemonade springs are placing their faith in technology in the same way their forebears placed their hopes in gold and silver mines and timber and canals full of blue water reaching out into the desert.

The dark side to this Chamber of Commerce-style optimism is that it can quickly turn into a belief in anything at all that will make a buck. The landscape of hope transforms into the balance sheet of hope, and the land stops being a place and starts being a clear-cut or a mine or a variation of Disneyland.

Writers can usually see this sort of thing before politicians or business people do, and I imagine Wallace Stegner finally saw that the people living in his landscape of hope had been motivated over the generations by nothing more than a money-grubbing nihilism.

NIETZSCHE MAY have had the American West and American Westerners in mind when he declared God dead in 1883. He wasn't announcing a celestial funeral. He simply meant that God, whether he existed or not, whether he was alive or not, was dead from the perspective of humans. God no longer had any claim on our imaginations or our behavior. Those who needed absolute proof that Nietzsche was right might have had to wait seven years, but here in the West, Wounded Knee did the trick.

When I assign Bill Joy's essay, I also assign "A Small Good Thing," a short story by Raymond Carver, written during his losing struggle with lung cancer. It's about the death of a child, and of people who found in a time of terrible tragedy a moment when they could break bread together. In that brief communion they discover their ability to care for each other, and in that caring they discover hope.

If we can see it, the real landscape of hope is already here. It's just on a smaller scale than we thought. There are small good things that we will find if we look closely at the sagebrush and sand and the dry mountains of the West.

But I don't think we'll be able to see those things until we've created a civilization where empathy for other people comes as a reflex, where we don't claim the sacred can be fenced off, and where we try to repair the damage that acting in our own narrow self-interest has done to the place where we live.

Then we might find we live in a place of communion and community. It'll be a place where we can grieve for all the dreams that have proven false.

In practical terms, it'll be a place where we make sure that everyone lives in decent housing, has enough to eat, and has medical care. It'll be a place where we clean up the messes of people who haven't cleaned up after themselves. It'll be a place where time is seen in terms of generations, and decisions are made for great-grandchildren. It'll be a place of small good things, because the big good things have all been used up, or killed off, or shown themselves not to be so good anymore.

For me, it means afternoons in the sauna, fishing when necessary to put food on the table, mornings planting trees, whole years spent listening to people who are older than I am tell their memories of what lies buried under the surface of our world. I've taken to working for an archaeologist in the summers, and the holes I dig for him have given me the idea that no place is real if it doesn't come equipped with its past. In the infinitely small moment of the present, all becomes uncertain and insubstantial. It takes time to know what's real and what isn't. It takes time to *become* real, and it takes time to understand the world's history well enough to write yourself into its future, which is, I think, what life in a landscape of hope is all about.

Rules for Writers

Ten Tips for Writing Yourself Back Into a Landscape of Hope

1. Recognize that if you lived in Eden, you wouldn't write a word. That guy with the flaming sword is your friend.

2. Avoid false hope.

3. Write history, not nostalgia.

4. Recognize that there's some magic in magical realism but none at all in magical thinking.

5. Don't shy away from grief.

6. Recognize your totem animal when it approaches you. Feed it and care for it, unless it's foaming at the mouth and snapping at you.

7. Following a story where it wants to go will usually take you to depths of your own heart.

8. Every draft takes a layer off the surface of your consciousness. Rewriting is a form of personal archaeology, and the good stuff is never on the surface.

9. Write toward the sacred. People die needing the sacred more than they need the material things they have acquired in place of the sacred.

10. Over time, your writing will become the place you live. Take good care of the furniture. Especially your chair.

6

The Writer as Witness

By good art I mean art that bears true witness.

—Ezra Pound

IN SEPTEMBER OF 1968, my parents loaded me and a suitcase and a new Smith-Corona portable typewriter in their car
and came down from the mountains of central Idaho to the town
of Caldwell, home of The College of Idaho. They took me to
Voorhees Hall on the college campus and left me there.

I was seventeen. I missed my girlfriend, even though we had
only started going out that July, had only decided we were in love
that August, and had only decided to get married as we had said
goodbye, forty-eight hours before. She was a fifteen-year-old
high-school sophomore and lived in Challis, six hours away on
the other side of the state. No matter how much we loved each
other, we faced logistics difficulties.

The minute my parents drove out of the Voorhees parking
lot, I missed them too, although if you had told me anytime
in the previous four years that I would miss my parents once I
finally got free of them I wouldn't have believed you.

There was a packet with my name on it in the lobby. It held a key to Room 101 and a list of house rules and a description of my roommate, who came from Shoshone, Idaho, an agricultural town 120 miles east of Caldwell on the Union Pacific rail line. Like me, he intended to major in psychology. He hadn't arrived yet.

I opened Room 101 and put my suitcase on the bed nearest the window. I set up my typewriter on the desk next to the bed, and on the bookshelf above it I placed the dictionary and desk encyclopedia my high-school guidance counselor had given me at graduation. Other books would join them soon, I knew. I had a checkbook and a hundred dollars in my account, and I knew enough about college to know that I would have to buy books, and that they were expensive, and that I'd be lucky to have fifty dollars when I walked out of the bookstore.

I was looking out the window onto the Voorhees lawn when there was a slow, heavy pounding on my door. I went to the door and opened it.

A six foot seven inch three hundred pound black man stood in my doorway. He was wearing shorts and flip-flops and a football jersey. He smiled down at me. I noticed he had a knife scar running across one cheek and over the bridge of his nose.

"My name is Ed Jones," he said. "I live in Room One-Oh-Two. You got any donuts?"

THESE DAYS I write and teach fiction. When I look at what I've put down here so far I can see that if it were the start of a short story, I'd have enough material already. Because there are too many characters, I'd have my roommate die in a train wreck on his way to college, and in one of the story's scenes Ed Jones and my fifteen-year-old girlfriend and I would go to my room-mate's memorial service at the college auditorium, a service held there because his noble but neurasthenic farming family—the Roderick Ushers of Shoshone—had sent its children there for four generations, and he was the last of the line. I would deliver an elegy that began, "I never knew my roommate, but I feel like I know him, because…" Ed Jones would go to the service because he was curious about death rituals in Idaho.

Afterward, Ed Jones and my girlfriend and I would buy a big box of donuts and a half gallon of Pepsi. We would go down to the railroad bridge a mile from campus and sit on the tracks. We would discuss the delicacy of life until the donuts and the Pepsi were gone. Then we all would go to the Caldwell City Hall and my girlfriend and I would get married. Ed Jones would be our witness. That's the story if I were writing fiction: a story about how arbitrarily a life can end, and about how the big moments of life require a witness.

BUT I'M NOT writing fiction. I'm trying to be a witness myself, forty years after the fact. Forty years brings so much truth into a story that you're lucky if you can comprehend it, much less tell it. Forty years turns the tragic into the comic. Life Goes turns into Life Goes On.

A few years ago I wrote a memoir, and joked in it that if by the age of fifty you get the face you deserve, a glance in the mirror tells me that I've sinned less than Keith Richards. It usually gets a laugh when I read it. The people in the audience that laugh the most are women in their fifties. Fifty-something women understand life doesn't often go according to plan. They understand it better than fifty-something men, some of whom still think that with a few weeks of training they could walk on to an NFL team, or that the twenty-year-old waitress who flirts with them in a restaurant really is charmed by their smile.

So here's what I've witnessed, or at least some of it: my roommate didn't die in a train wreck because his sturdy-looking parents drove him from Shoshone by car. As far as I know, nobody in his family ever had a farm or money, and in the rocky soil of Shoshone, money and farms have never gone together anyway.

My roommate still hasn't graduated from The College of Idaho because of a couple of courses he never found the time to take. He also started drinking too much. He hasn't had a drink in decades, but still calls himself an alcoholic. He met a nice woman in an Alcoholics Anonymous meeting and married her. She has a good job as a state biologist, and he runs a landscape business.

Given where he was forty years ago, he is wealthy and happy and lucky. He's evidence that if you learn from sad experience, it's not the end of the world if you don't finish those last few classes. It's not always the end of the world if you become an alcoholic, either, although it is the end of the person you thought you were before you started drinking. We ask alcohol to change who we are, but often enough that change comes only after a despairing night-sea journey. It's one more example of why we should be careful what we ask for.

My roommate and I kept a supply of donuts in Room 101 for when Ed Jones came by, and he came by often. I hadn't known any black people when I was growing up, but I had been damaged by racism in my high school and at my family dinner table. Ed was kind enough to tell two small-town Idaho kids what it had been like to grow up in a tough neighborhood in Washington, D.C., and how we couldn't go home with him for Thanksgiving because of our race. It was the first time we had ever thought of our race as a liability.

At The College of Idaho, however, we could all break bread together—deep fat fried bread, covered with sugar—and my roommate and I received an education in humanity and empathy from Ed, a man who was willing to talk about racism to people who had no idea how much it had shaped their world and caused them to be the people they were.

Ed Jones died of cancer ten years ago. He had graduated from The College of Idaho, and he became a parole officer in California. He worked with hurt and angry people until a few months before he died. I like to think that he helped them to heal by showing them what he had shown us: that humanity and decency and a simple communion can replace fear and ignorance with respect and affection.

My girlfriend broke up with me by Christmas of my freshman year. She had started going out with a guy on the wrestling team of her small high school. In the spring of that year he was killed in a car accident, and in May I started getting letters from her again. We went out that next summer. I fell in love with her again, but by Christmas of my sophomore year she broke up with me and married somebody else.

By then I had left The College of Idaho and was in the middle of a cold winter in Cambridge, Massachusetts. I had transferred to Harvard, and hadn't made many friends there, and when my girlfriend told me goodbye I almost died. For many years I thought she had a mean streak, but when I finally met her over coffee a few years ago I understood that what I had thought was a mean streak was just a core of loneliness. Loneliness had made her fall out of love with me and get married to someone else and raise a couple of kids, and through all of that time her loneliness had kept itself intact in her heart. Having coffee with her made me feel lonely myself.

WITNESSING is a terrifying assumption of responsibility, especially when it involves memory. You look back at your own life and see that you made life-and-death decisions without knowing anything about life and death. Theoretical physicists tell us that every time we make a choice we create not just a new self but a new universe. Other selves in other universes exist because we made different choices.

In another universe, I graduated from The College of Idaho with a psychology degree. I'd like to talk to that version of myself, to see how well he got to know Ed Jones, and if in his universe Ed is still alive and if he's a parole officer or something else. It occurs to me that Ed would have made a good psychotherapist, because he was smart and tough and compassionate and funny. Maybe, in most universes, he didn't get cancer. Maybe in one of them he is a psychotherapist and so am I, and we've opened a psychotherapy practice together, and we always have lots of clients because we're smart and funny and compassionate and in the waiting room of our office there's always a big box of donuts.

This particular self—the one addressing you now—became a teacher of writing. My job tends to magnify people's emotional problems instead of reduce them. You can't ask people to spend huge portions of their lives staring at mostly blank screens, waiting for the sentence that will make meaning out of chaos, without expecting them to go a little nuts. You also can't ask them to look carefully at and tell the truth about this world and its history and not expect them to find, engrained in their hearts, a terrible anger.

AT THE COLLEGE OF IDAHO I switched to English Literature in my first semester. In the middle of the second semester I applied to transfer to Harvard, and that summer they accepted me. By May of 1972, thanks to a government that would have sent me to Vietnam if I had dropped out of college, I was a Harvard graduate. If that sounds impressive, you probably have some other Harvard graduate in mind.

When I was accepted at Harvard, I thought it was because Harvard liked my SAT scores. I later found out that they liked my history. When I was born, my parents lived in a mining camp. I had gone to a two-room school in the first grade. My father had made his living as a miner and trapper and hunting guide. They didn't have anyone remotely like me at Harvard. I was accepted as an anthropological specimen.

I did have one skill that the Harvard admissions committee wanted. My writing class at The College of Idaho had taught me about writing simple, short sentences and assembling them into coherent paragraphs. It had taught me to use the dictionary that my counselor had given me, and it taught me to go to the library and research the papers I wrote.

One final reason I was accepted was that my application essay was about my widening vision of the world. I had gone from a two-room schoolhouse to The College of Idaho to Harvard. The implication was that Harvard was to The College of

Idaho as The College of Idaho was to a two-room schoolhouse. The admissions committee found that comparison believable.

Harvard really thought it was as wide as the world could get. It looked favorably on anyone smart enough to see that.

But The College of Idaho was a more spacious place than I thought, and Harvard was narrower. I used the writing skills I learned at The College of Idaho to coast through my time at Harvard. I found I could write a paper for almost any class, and because I could write well, I'd get an A or B.

Since that time, I've learned that if you can write well, people believe what you say, because there's an implicit cultural understanding that when you write something down, it's like having an extra brain out there. If the writing is going well, what you're thinking is on the page in front of you, and it's better thinking than you could ever do if it was still stuck in your frontal lobes.

There's a dark side to this phenomenon. After spending a couple of decades teaching college, I know now that my professors at Harvard were so grateful to have a student who could write that they didn't care what I thought.

There's another dark side to this phenomenon. A parole officer sits at a desk late at night, catching up on his reports. He's a good writer, but his writing is acting like an extra brain, and what that extra brain is thinking is that his simple strong sentences and coherent paragraphs have made him a credible witness. His job is such that what he writes as a witness keeps some people in prison and sets other people free. It's not a responsibility he was asking for when he signed up for Freshman Composition at The College of Idaho.

SOMETIMES DIVERGENT universes reconnect, and two of them reconnected in my first semester at Harvard, while I was waiting in a line of work-study students in the Harvard Union. The guy next to me was black. Earlier that month a group of black students had taken over the Administration Building for a couple of days. The Harvard Administration was puzzled and hurt that their gift of a white man's education hadn't been accepted with gratitude and humility. There was a lot of anger in the air, and not a lot of talk between people of different races. But I was from Idaho, and lonely, and I didn't know any better than to talk to the guy next to me.

"So were you in the Administration Building takeover?" I asked him.

It was a question that told him I was only seeing his skin. The reality was more complicated, and had to do with missing The College of Idaho, and Ed Jones, and donuts, but it would have been impossible for me to explain all that.

He looked at me like I was an idiot, which I was.

"Where you from, anyway?" he asked.

"Idaho," I said.

"Explains a lot," he said.

"Where you from?" I asked.

"Washington, D.C.," he said.

"You know Ed Jones?" I asked.

His mouth fell open. "Big Ed Jones?"

"Goes to The College of Idaho?" I asked.

He turned to the black guy next to him and said, "He knows Ed Jones."

"No," said the other guy. "He doesn't know Ed Jones."

"I know Ed Jones," I said. And then I told them about arriving at The College of Idaho, and about the donuts, and transferring to Harvard, and how Ed had told me he came from a tough neighborhood in D.C. They agreed that Ed's neighborhood was tough. But they said Ed was tougher. Nobody messed with Ed Jones. I told them Ed was one of the nicest, gentlest guys I had ever met.

They had been looking at me like I was stupid. Now they looked at me like I was crazy.

THE THREE OF US, because of our position in the work-study line, ended up mopping the floors in the freshman dining hall every morning at 6 a.m. Work-study—lots of it—was the only way we could afford college. We became cautious friends, which is to say that on the job, we helped each other out when we could and nobody left before the job was finished. If one of us missed a day we did his work without complaining. But we didn't have much in common other than knowing Ed Jones, and relations between the races at Harvard stayed toxic.

The next year my work-study job was working in Widener Library, the giant archive at the center of Harvard Yard. In the dining hall, I had worked with political science majors. At the circulation desk, everybody on the all-white crew was studying literature and philosophy and psychology. I never saw my co-workers from the dining hall again.

AT CONVOCATION at Middlebury College, which is isolated in the dark center of Vermont, the president used to tell new students to look around at their classmates. "You're probably looking at your spouse," the Middlebury president told them. "Two out of three of you will marry another Middlebury student."

While that statistic is false—the actual proportion is closer to twenty percent—it still means that of all the wonderful people on the planet that each Middlebury student could marry, the one a big share of them will pick is a person who kept them warm in the middle of a miserable cold night in Vermont in January.

It's not just Middlebury. At my own high school graduation, the mother of one of my classmates asked me why I was going to The College of Idaho. I was going there because my guidance counselor had insisted on it. Beyond that I didn't have a clue. I was just going to college, because my family told me that it was my next step after high school. When you're seventeen years old, almost everyone you deal with is telling you to do something, whether they have your best interests in mind or not.

"I don't know why I'm going to The College of Idaho," I told my classmate's mother.

"You will," she said, "when you meet Mrs. John Rember there."

I determined at that moment never to marry anyone I met at The College of Idaho. For that matter, I determined never to get married. It was 1968, and people my age had figured out that marriage was not necessary. We were in a new era of freedom and love. Spending your life yoked to another person meant taking on an unnecessary burden.

But I am married now, and I met my wife Julie at The College of Idaho. We met in September of 1989, when I was teaching my first class there, and Julie was *taking* her first class there. We joke to each other that we bonded like baby ducks, falling in love with the first person we saw as we broke out of the egg, but it wasn't like that. We got together much later, after we discovered that we had both grown up on isolated ranches, away from towns and organized social lives, and that our worlds had kept getting larger and more complicated all through our lives, even when we didn't want them to. We saw in our marriage a safe place, one where the operative words were kindness and trust and continuity.

I've come to see my classmate's mother as someone who bestowed a blessing instead of a curse, and I hope that those Middlebury students who marry each other find the same sort of deepening refuge from those dark winter nights.

IF I HAD NEVER been married to Julie I wouldn't be able to even think about Ed Jones now. I'll explain, but before I do, let me also explain that in another universe, I really am a psychotherapist. He's a sadder person than the person I am. I can joke about comedy being tragedy plus time, but he deals with people who have managed to stop time at the bound moment of grief.

His clients have taken a wound in their lives and turned it into so much scar tissue that they can't move. They see their own immobility as evidence that they've stopped the universe from expanding into empty and ever-colder space, and stopped their own relentless march toward old age and death. Bent, crabbed, barely able to walk, they spend their days keeping this universe and their lives within it the only way things could have worked out.

When these clients hobble into my other-me's office, he offers them a donut. They always refuse it. "A donut is a good thing," he says. "Why say no to a good thing?" And so therapy begins.

My other-me attempts to create a *temenos* with his clients. A *temenos*, in psychotherapy, means a constructed space—a container—inside which a client and therapist can trust each other. Inside a *temenos*, people can think anything and say anything. They can follow tearful effect back to cruel cause. Inside the container, the forbidden sentence can be spoken, and the forbidden thought can come to consciousness.

In classical Greece, *temenos* meant a place in a temple, usually a well-demarcated space around an altar, within which your own divine spark could connect with its wellsprings. When psychotherapy goes well, the two meanings of *temenos* merge. People are born out of that sacred space into a world where time hasn't been stopped, a world that no longer profanes innocence, a world that still contains an accessible divine, a world where a long healing can begin.

So the other-universe me that is a psychotherapist spends a lot of time trying to establish a trust with people who have spent most of their lives betraying people before anyone has a chance to betray them first.

As I said, he's a sadder man than I am.

When Julie and I met, I was twenty years older than she was, street smart, and as a member of a small college faculty, accustomed to using my critical intelligence as a weapon. The chances of the two of us creating a safe place between us were slim and none. There must be thousands of universes where we met and wounded each other and moved on, angrier and more betrayed, to wound others.

But in this universe we're coming up on twenty years of being kind to each other, of non-betrayal, of the deliberate suspension of street smarts, of taking care of the space that we have created around us. And even though I've said it's a container, it's a container where space opens infinitely inward, where possibilities multiply, and where, for me at least, all the angers and treacheries of the greater world can be seen as minor and transient. It's not a bad thing to have rage and treachery grow smaller with the application of time and consciousness and the discovery of previously unknown spaces within.

In other universes I have not been so lucky. A few years ago, I had an all-too-lucid dream where I realized that I was sitting behind the steering wheel of a wrecked car. I was drunk. Every bone in my upper body had been broken. I had hit a wall, or a bridge abutment, or another car head-on. I was dying all alone in this dream, and I remember knowing that death was coming, and welcoming it as the end of a pain far greater than the physical.

I tell my writing students never, ever to write my next sentence: Then I woke up.

I was in my own familiar bed. Julie was sleeping beside me, making soft little snores. I was uninjured, sober, and safe, and nothing was broken. In at least one other universe, that sense of being far away and intact was just the last flaming hallucination of dying brain cells.

ED JONES never used the word *temenos* in our late-night dorm room discussions. But he knew how to construct one, because he consciously got rid of his street smarts whenever we talked. That's hard to do when your street smarts have been survival skills.

I never knew what street Ed Jones grew up on, but I've been to tough neighborhoods in Washington, D.C. I've seen bars on the windows of the houses and piles of garbage on the sidewalks and broken buildings and broken people sitting on the curbs. I've seen young men with street smarts glowing like klieg lights in their eyes. I've thought that when they looked at me they saw a human shape, washed-out, ghostlike, reduced to a blank outline, barely there, white beyond any concept of whiteness. Behind it, a bleached blur of sky, and just the hint of the shadows of buildings and trees. It's a scene from an overexposed world. It's a world where nothing is as it appears. It's a world where trust is impossible.

So in that universe where I'm a psychotherapist, I try to emulate Ed Jones and get rid of my street smarts when I'm starting out with a client. And I never bring up the claustrophobic concept of a container.

That's because a deliberately-created container that opens inward and where people soften the boundaries between themselves and others—that also describes the families my clients are supposed to have grown up in. Except these families have been prisons instead of safe houses. People wouldn't be sitting in my office using up my boxes of alternate-reality Kleenex if someone close to them hadn't violated their boundaries, abused their trust, and forced them into lonely internal exile.

Without trust and good will and love, a family or marriage or job becomes the container from hell. The one trusted with power turns into a vampire. The safe place turns into a torture chamber. Community turns to tribalism turns to racism turns to scapegoating turns to murder turns to genocide.

My alternate self tries to form a relationship with each client where betrayal isn't the norm and where the truth is told as often as we both can stand, and where the escape hatch is always open.

In 1968, Ed Jones must have known that some of life's containers could be lethal. He also must have known that with care, you could consciously construct a safe place. In the face of my near-total lack of street smarts, he didn't react with scorn or cruelty. It must have gone against all his cultural training to see me as a human being worthy of respect. It must have taken great courage for him to treat me as a person capable of understanding and friendship, as someone who wouldn't jump at the chance to betray him before he could betray me first.

WHEN I BEGIN working with a new writing student, I tell her that we're not doing psychotherapy. What we're doing is far more important than psychotherapy. Your writing is going to make the world a better place, I tell her. You're going to be a witness for mute and suffering people who lack your ability to perceive. And your words, when you bring them to your perceptions, are not going to lie to or betray anyone.

If my student believes me, chances are good that her writing will cross a threshold into a deep and painful place. Lots of those mute and suffering people live on the inside, and writing is the one thing that will let us cross into their territory.

"You don't have to live there," I say about the far side of that frightening threshold. "But you have to be able to go there. You have to be able to get back. Maybe you won't have to go to that same place again. Maybe you will, but at least you'll know the second time that you can survive it."

It's taken forty years, but I now realize that Ed Jones was a writer writing his own life, following his story where it led, and crossing thresholds into deadly territory. He was going to college in a country where the deliberately focused terror of the lynch mob was still, in 1968, an instrument of domestic policy. Black eighteen-year-olds who couldn't afford college went to Vietnam because it was safer than staying home. The 1964 Watts riots and the 1967 Detroit riots and the King assassination were fresh in the nation's memory. People who looked like Ed Jones were being used to frighten white people into voting for the racist demagogue George Wallace, and the tactics of racial politics left few safe places for anybody of any race.

Yet by accepting a football scholarship at a liberal arts college in an overwhelmingly white state, and ensuring that he, too, was going to go through college as an anthropological specimen, Ed Jones took the risk that he could, in an isolated small town deep in the desert West, create a safe place for himself. He took the risk that such a safe place could include someone—me—who was too naïve to know how valuable a safe place could be. He was gambling that my lack of street smarts, my ignorance of the brutality of American history, my undamaged faith in true love and my complacent belief in my own bright future—he was trusting that these things were worth protecting from destruction until I could balance them with their opposites, drawn from hard experience in the world.

A brave story. And it became braver still, when Ed Jones went on to assume that I was smart enough to forgive him for consciously creating the container that held us both safe for the few months of the school year of 1968-1969. He had faith in the person I would become, the one able to understand why he might practice psychotherapy without a license.

In yet another alternate universe, Ed Jones is a writer, not a psychotherapist, and I'm his character, a creature of his imagination. I'm not sure the alternate universe isn't this one, and that these words aren't being written because he was able to imagine me writing them.

ED JONES the writer. Ed Jones the psychotherapist. It's obvious now that Ed Jones plays a greater role in my imagination than in my memory. Ed Jones is a part of a universe lost to my experience when I applied to Harvard. He represents a psychology degree from The College of Idaho and recalls the myriad small decisions that took me universes away from the one where I once broke bread with him.

In some of those universes, I'm dead and Ed Jones is alive. In some of those universes, he's my parole officer. I have married half a dozen, a hundred, a thousand different women in those universes, and maybe some gentle and kind men. Quantum physics can make you the ultimate polygamist, the ultimate chameleon, the person with a million different disguises, a billion different identities. I think of Ed Jones and I think of multitudes.

I'm playing with metaphor here, which is a dangerous thing to do. I tell my writing students to be careful of metaphors, whether they look like Ed Jones or not. Preconceptions are learning disabilities, I tell them, and everything that comes after metaphor is preconception. Good stories are ruined because the metaphor takes over and you have to trim characters and events to fit it. Metaphors damage your ability just to witness the world.

I tell my students metaphors are the Procrustean Bed of

writers. Often enough they will point out that a Procrustean Bed is a metaphor. I just grin at them.

Then I say that you have to take apart the metaphors, go back to what they were before they became metaphors, and when you do you'll find stories. For example, Procrustes wasn't always someone who chopped off the feet of his guests or stretched them to fit his furniture.

Before he did that, he was an abused little kid whose parents short-sheeted his bed and gave him full-size footballs before he could get his hands around them and who was a miserable ordinary C student in junior high and high school. The A students picked on him in class and the F students beat him up after school, and his guidance counselor called him mediocre and recommended that he go to a junior college and study computer repair instead of telling him he had to go to The College of Idaho or Harvard. Those sorts of things can make you bitter and lonely. When you get a little power over innocent and trusting people, you do terrible things to them, just to satisfy that little core of loneliness in your heart.

IF I LOOK at the story of my life as I would a student's story, I see that I dropped a huge metaphor into it when I left The College of Idaho and became a Harvard student. I stopped paying attention to what I was seeing and started preconceiving my experience. Harvard students were guaranteed good jobs and were smarter than other people—because they'd been accepted by what they had been told was the best university in the country. That made me one of the best university students in the country.

I stopped being a witness. I didn't pay enough attention to

my fellow students to know that very few of them were as smart as Ed Jones or my College of Idaho roommate, or that few of them could write. I didn't pay much attention during lectures. I skipped classes, knowing that my final twenty-page written-the-night-before-it-was-due paper would be good enough to get me yet another B+ for the semester.

It wasn't until ten years later, when I was a medical writer interviewing physicians in Boston, that I got back to Harvard. In the middle of Harvard Square I decided that the big change that had happened since I had left was that there were all these arrogant assholes walking around. But nothing had changed. I was just seeing what Harvard undergraduates look like from the outside.

Now, when anyone finds out that I went to Harvard, I explain to them that it took decades, but that Harvard has worn off and I'm back to normal. Some people see that as an arrogant statement, but what I mean is that I have gone back to the way I perceived things before I was buried in an Ivied wall, and I'm gradually resurrecting my experience and witnessing my life. It's much harder to do this way than it would have been for me to just look around the first time, stop and listen in quiet places, and feel the texture of each moment.

The second time through it's a kind of personal archaeology, an opening of lost tombs. You know there was a rich civilization there, but all you hold in your hand are bones, and bronze, and tarnished jewels.

A CONCEPT increasingly useful in our culture is penance. Penance is a way of being that allows you to unburden yourself of mistakes you've made. Often, you spend a long time doing penance for mistakes that took only a short time to commit.

My penance for leaving The College of Idaho before I finished what I had begun there was that I ended up teaching writing in its classrooms for fifteen years.

During that time I tried to teach my students to be witnesses. I tried to teach them the relationship between experience and language, and to put experience first to the extent that they could. I taught them to go easy on the metaphors, because metaphors are like salmon fillets: if you forget that last grocery bag and leave them in the car over a couple of hot August afternoons, they'll become hard to live with.

I asked my writing students to be open to the story that found them from the inside, and to listen carefully to the still, small voice of the story when they were stuck and the words wouldn't come. I told them that metaphors fly at thirty thousand feet, drinking martinis in a Lear jet and seeing whole cities as webs of light, but stories crawl along muddy ground on their bellies, getting insect bites and bruises, trying to sneak up close enough to get a glimpse of something small and shining and so rare that there's only one of it in all the world.

During those fifteen years I learned what I should have learned the first time at The College of Idaho: to be as kind as I can to the people around me, to respect their innocence as evidence that the world hasn't always been cruel to everybody, to never see myself or other people as walking metaphors, to pull language toward the tangible and the blunt and the literal.

Together, those things have created a universe, and it's as close to the universe that came through my door at The College of Idaho as long years of enormous and deliberate acts of will could make it. I wish Ed Jones were still here to witness it with me.

Rules for Writers

Ed Jones's Ten Truths that Will Help You Be a Better Writer by Being a Better Witness

1. If you're white, don't assume you can know what it's like to be a black person. If you're black, don't assume you can know what it's like to be white. The same caution applies to all races, genders, occupations, educations, and levels of wealth.

2. Experience trumps language.

3. Don't pride yourself on your empathy. You have less than you think you have. Most of the time what you think is empathy is projection, where you assume that someone else's inside is just like your inside, warts and all. It's not. People who have been married for twenty years sometimes look at each other and discover they have no idea who the other person is.

4. Being in love with or hating characters makes getting to know them exponentially more difficult.

5. Your characters are real, but they're not flesh and blood people. From the standpoint of your readers, they're words on a page that they hope to be able to use to imagine flesh and blood people.

6. Street smarts don't always work on the page. For example, I've wondered what it would have been like for Ed Jones to have so much physical and emotional and intellectual power, and to have found a place where he could express it freely— The College of Idaho—and then go out into the world as a

cog in a great prison system whose greatest purpose, if you look at the evidence, is to keep poor black and brown people locked up. What's it like to be a superior human being who becomes a self-betraying functionary in an inferior and corrupt system? More people than Ed Jones have found out. That's street smarts talking, and the bad thing about street smarts is that they close off possibilities, in stories and in life. They will make your writing into a self-contained, self-reinforcing system, and that's a form of self-inflicted blindness. I'm not saying that street smarts can't get at the truth. They just don't tell very good stories.

7. If you write down overheard dialogue and what you see when you sit for an hour in a coffee shop and stare at people's faces, you'll likely upset people and maybe get arrested. But you'll be a better writer.

8. The code of conduct for a witness starts with paying careful attention to what's going on around you, and avoiding making assumptions based on preconception or prejudice.

9. It's possible to subject memory to the available evidence. There's always opportunity for fact checking, even in fiction.

10. If you'll open the door when somebody's pounding on it, the stories will find you.

7

Writing Image

Some ships sail from their ports, and ever afterwards are missing.
—Herman Melville

I'M WALKING along a river. It's swollen with spring runoff, and as I'm wading through flooded riverbank grass I look ahead to a crowd of people clustered at the side of a bridge. I get closer and see that they're looking at a body wrapped around one of the pilings. When I get to the crowd I ask who has drowned. Somebody says it's Ernest Hemingway.

Hemingway looks awful. Fish have eaten off his nose and his flesh has the clean translucence of death-by-washing. His eyes have turned to black oil behind lids not quite shut. He's wearing a khaki safari suit that's growing green moss where the current isn't hitting it and waving long skeins of thread where it is. His feet are bare and broken, missing toes and trailing tendons. As I watch, a cheek falls open, exposing teeth, and I understand that Hemingway is grinning at me. I am unable to look away. For a moment I don't know if the assessing gaze belongs to me or to him.

Then I look around in the crowd, look back at Hemingway,

and say to everybody, "Well, he looks like he's got at least one more book in him."

Then I wake up, terrified but laughing, because what I've said is funny to a writer who has trouble making a living at it but who has watched the posthumous production of bestsellers out of Hemingway's wastebasket.

I get out of bed and wrap myself in a robe. The image of the drowned writer stays with me even as I understand that some voice within me can make a joke about anything, no matter how filled with grief, no matter how grotesque, no matter how filled with horror. I turn the kitchen light on and go to the sink to get a glass of water and a couple of aspirin, and my face reflected in the dark window now looks like a skull. I grin at myself in recognition. "Well, it looks like you've got at least one more book in you," I say.

I go back in the bedroom and go back to sleep and don't dream again about Hemingway. By mid-morning my thinking is crowded with words and I don't remember the nightmare until I wonder, in the middle of reading a story by a talented young student, where that talent and youth have come from. The dead Hemingway is suddenly all I see. I remember how I dealt with it with words and how once the words were there I could gaze at the image without being taken into those black eyes and that grinning, half-decayed head.

A THOUGHT EXPERIMENT: It's 1979, and you're an unemployed young high-school dropout in a garage band. Since the Dead Kennedys name is already taken, you call yourself the Dead Hemingways. You pierce your lips and cheeks and forehead with Royal Coachmen and Renegades and White Ghosts.

Your first big hit is "Jake Ain't Got It And Lady Brett Never Had It," and it consists of those same words repeated forty-two times to a two-chord guitar riff.

You quickly get an underground reputation for nasty behavior onstage. In the middle of songs, you take out your fly rod and whip the people jumping up and down in the mosh pit, whip them good, really good, so that at the end of the evening, when your music has been head-banging loud for long enough and your wrist action skilled enough, and the fly lines have left enough bloody tracks on bare skin, everybody will have broken the bonds of the physical, will have broken on through to where the real dead Hemingways, the suicidal quintet of Ernest and his granddaughter Margaux and his father and his brother and his sister, whip themselves with their own fly rods, like medieval penitents. They nod to you and go back to their business.

It's a vision of hell, and in it you find reason enough to quit the band and get a job writing technical manuals for Microsoft, which turns out to be a move too far in the other direction, which is why you're thinking about becoming a writer. Writing's yet another extreme, but you think it might give you some sort of handle on the whipsaw of life.

Yet you're worried, because those bloody nights onstage taught you to be careful of what you do in this life because everything we do here exists in ironic counterpart on the other side. You don't have to know too many of the working writers who killed themselves to know that the other side can come much too alive for writers, and pull them through the mirror once the lights go out.

SO HOW DID we get here? A few paragraphs into a chapter on the craft of writing, we're in a vaster and bleaker place, one ruled over by grim majestic Hades and his half-time queen Persephone, who, now that she's acquired a taste for pomegranate juice, kind of likes being queen of the dead. Surrounding her is a retinue of suicidal writers: Hemingway and Sylvia Plath and Anne Sexton. John Kennedy O'Toole. Malcolm Lowry. David Foster Wallace and Jerzy Kosinski. Hart Crane. Faulkner, drinking himself to death. John Berryman. And they've all got one more book in them. It's based on that one last bright thing they saw in the world above, before the crack opened between their feet and strong fingers wrapped around their ankles.

When the Greek hero Hercules visited Hades, the shades of the dead clustered around him, begging him for his blood. With a drop of living blood they could gain substance and go back to the world and revenge themselves upon their enemies. Hercules refused them, understanding that if he gave one drop of blood he would end up sucked dry by the brooding, obsessive, vengeance-seeking shades who thickened the air around him. If Hercules hadn't visited the warrior section of Hades, but had instead gone to see Persephone's stable of writers, he no doubt would have been asked for blood so that a bunch of unfinished manuscripts could be completed.

HADES AND ITS HOST of images—not all of them ghosts, as even the rocks there have stories for us—have a special place in the life of all writers, not just the writers who have killed themselves. And it's not just because we can sometimes see the words on the wall above our writing desk that read Abandon

Hope, All Ye Who Enter Here.

It's because writers more or less constantly mediate between language and nightmare—nightmare that can't be traced to childhood trauma, or the death of a loved one, or the monster movie you just saw. It instead comes into your sleep from an inhuman world. It fills completely the screen of your mind and you wake up throwing words at it in order to bring narrative to something that exists outside of time. Writing is a kind of dreaming while armed with language, and when you write you're subject to the same invasion from the inhuman, the same necessity to name and date the unnamable and undateable and thereby save yourself, just like you have to sometimes save yourself with words when you're having a nightmare.

You can save yourself because image and language are not even close to the same thing, although it's tempting to think so when we see a phrase like "flower in the crannied wall." Those words create a picture in our mind, but also an illusion that words are pictures.

Words aren't pictures. Words are words—when they're not the thick insulation in which desperate writers wrap images when the images get too scary.

Not-so-desperate writers reverse the process. They reduce language and sometimes destroy it to deliberately travel toward a risky and uncomfortable place: the one where holes in the language let us walk toward shapes we cannot grasp and toward images which, if they grasp us, will devour us.

In practical terms, that's one of the reasons that if you cut a story's first draft by 25 percent, it will become better, more intense, and smarter. More will be at stake. It will have more meaning to your reader than it did in its self-indulgent fullness, and much of that increase of meaning is the decrease in the amount of insulation from the real those extra words provided.

Laboring with language to explain a scene in cinematic fullness is a process that can attenuate rather than concentrate meaning. You have to have something to destroy in the first place, but that's what first drafts are for. As any blue-pencil-wielding editor knows, destroying language doesn't only concentrate meaning but in a sense makes it possible. You just have to know what to leave in and what to leave out.

It's why a good editor is both the writer's worst enemy and best friend. For those of us who lack a Maxwell Perkins, that worst enemy and best friend have to reside in our own skull, and we hope that they exchange ambassadors.

LANGUAGE BY ITSELF is insubstantial—like shades in Hades—but if you wound it and give it a drop of its own blood, it can suddenly act in the world.

It should be clear that deliberately crafted word pictures are not what I'm talking about here. You can play with language and images are sometimes the result. Careers have been consciously constructed out of word play. Gertrude Stein did well with phrases like Tender Buttons, but those whimsically connected words are not what make her a dangerous and powerful writer. Rather, it's her ability to use repetition and incongruity to destroy language, to knock a hole in the playground fence, and to beckon us outside, to where the dark shapes lurk.

I'M MAKING some assumptions here that are not universal among writing teachers. The largest of these assumptions is that the image is the world and language exists in some external relation to it—or, put another way, image is primary and language is secondary. A good many language theorists who also teach people to write believe that language exists to the exclusion of everything else—language is reality—and as long as they can stay sequestered inside university English departments, little will cause them to question that world view.

But as a writer, I've always been fond of the scene in *Raiders of the Lost Ark* where Indiana Jones, threatened by a master swordsman and skilled martial artist, pulls out a pistol and shoots him dead. That's a refutation of those folks who say that without language, we wouldn't be able to think, wouldn't be conscious, wouldn't be able to live in a reality because outside of language there is only dark and mute electrochemical reaction. Indiana Jones's pistol gives the lie to all those decades of close combat training and mental discipline, and to all those PhDs in literary theory.

The uncomfortable conclusion here is that the world is true and language is false. But all of us who have struggled to put the truth into words know that language has to be tricked into telling the truth and into reconnecting with the image that gave rise to it. Turned away from image, language will lie by comfortable omission. As writers, that's one of the paths open to us, and few of us can resist the temptation to take it. When a story isn't working for me, I always go through my most recent draft to find the point where I began to lie by omission.

WHEN I WAS TEACHING English composition, I would assign a one-page autobiography on the first day of class. It was a way of assessing who was a good writer and who was not, and who was thoughtful and self-conscious as a first-year college student—and who was not. But it was also a way of showing my students that language has a relationship to the real but never is reality.

"You can't tell the truth about yourself in one page," I would say when I handed the papers back, and I'd demonstrate by having them read their papers aloud for a small amount of easy credit in the class. Some of them wouldn't read those pages for any amount of offered credit, because they were in effect introducing themselves to their peers with the same words they had chosen to introduce themselves to their professor.

They had lied. They had used language as foundation makeup, the base layer for a persona that was designed to get an A in English comp.

Such lying is not restricted to students. Look at what those of us in academia have done with our vitas, academic papers, syllabi, letters of recommendation, and committee reports. You can make a life of those things. You can use them to build an image of yourself but it will eventually go feral and eat your soul.

You can still live without a soul. In place of a soul you will have an underwater mortgage and car payments and tenure evaluations.

I hope what I'm doing with the language right now shows a different relationship to language, one that preserves a writer's soul, even if it involves blowing a hole in the language playground's fence and going to see the folks who have been lurking out there in the shadows.

If the world is real and language less so, language needs to be subverted if you're doing your job as a writer.

If you are just beginning to write, and even if you have been writing for years, these may be discouraging words. Giving over a huge part of your life to language—becoming a writer—requires faith in language. But that faith cannot be naïve if you want to be a good writer. A faith based on the idea that language cannot be true may not look like faith at all, but if it backs up an awareness that language is our only defense against the power of the image, it will be foxhole faith, the strongest, least naïve, and best kind of faith of all.

I'M THE WRITER AT LARGE for The College of Idaho, a small liberal arts college in Caldwell, Idaho, thirty miles outside of Boise. My duties involve talking to high school students, and one early May morning I got caught in a freeway traffic jam between Caldwell and Boise and came to a dead stop on I-84 about ten miles from the nearest Boise exit. I listened to National Public Radio, switched to an oldies station, checked my watch and saw that I would still be on time if traffic re-started in a half-hour or so, because I had planned on this traffic jam. I switched back to NPR, listened to the same program I had a half-hour earlier, and wished I'd bought a paper. Then I started looking at the cars around me and the people in them.

Image imposed itself on my vision. Instead of seeing stuck commuters in Boise, Idaho, I saw the *Terminator 2* post-holocaust freeway scene, where miles of stalled and burned cars are filled with fleshless human skeletons. There on I-84, without a movie theater for miles, I looked around me and saw no one who wasn't dead.

If you think this is just crazy, remember that the George Romero movie *Dawn of the Dead* used actual footage from shopping mall security cameras when they needed flesh-eating zombie crowd scenes. "Why are they here?" asks one of the few living characters in the film, watching the zombies on video monitors in the mall's control center. "Instinct. Memory," replies another. "This was an important place in their lives."

I GOT TO Timberline High School on time. Things went well until I took a question from a student asking why he should give up his freedom and go to college. It's a good question, if you're a senior in high school with ten days to go until graduation. Sometimes being Writer at Large and talking to these audiences is tough duty.

But it was the wrong question to ask a Writer at Large suffering from Interstate Terminator Movie hallucinations.

"Freedom?" I asked him. "Freedom?" And then I told about the traffic jam and all the dead people I had seen and that probably there wasn't any way for him to avoid being dead in a car someday in the middle of a bunch of other dead people who just think they're alive.

The sad thing is these high-school seniors all knew what I was talking about. They'd all seen *Terminator 2*. When I brought up the image, I looked out at a bunch of fresh young faces and saw the shock of recognition—the shock coming when they saw that an adult could think about things this way instead of giving them a pep talk about being at the threshold of a wonderful adventure.

They knew all this stuff already. It's a pretty heavy thing to know when you're seventeen, especially when you're not so good with the language that you can construct narratives in the face of the images nuclear war brings.

"Go to college," I said. "Maybe you can put off death for another four years."

OF COURSE there are other reasons to go to college and other reasons to learn to write—although putting off death isn't a bad reason to learn to write. Lots of people become writers to save their lives, and that's a far better reason to be a writer than wanting to become successful and published. It's good if you can do both, but first things first.

When I talk to people about the value of learning to write, I try to explain the difficulty of becoming a good writer on your own. I say that if you are really talented and choose to go it alone, without the benefit of the experience of all of the thousands of writers who have gone before you, for a long time you're going to write like Grandma Moses paints. You'll be a charming primitive.

A philosophical way to put this problem is that you might start out optimistic and pragmatic and with the assumption that there are a limited number of techniques to learn and once you learn them, you'll be a writer. But after you've been such a writer for a while, particularly if you're not making a lot of money at it, you'll start thinking about the big picture of human aspiration and where you fit in it. Then you'll start to consider the impossibility and absurdity of bringing order and narrative to a chaotic and disconnected world. You may stop at that point.

But it's hard to throw away these skills once you've got them. You'll probably start writing again, if only for the sake of making your abject failures into magnificent failures.

The newly skilled writer thinks that experience, once transformed into language, will lead to a narrative that gives him a place in a human world and places the world in time. The loose ends all get tied up.

The older and wiser writer recognizes that there are more loose ends than he could ever tie up, and what's more, they want to switch places with him—they want to tie him up. Work gets finished but the world it was supposed to change remains as chaotic and as inhuman and as messy as ever, and unbidden visions begin to creep into the controlled sanctity of the writing studio. They flicker in the margins of computer monitors. Strange scenes appear in the frames of dust-frosted basement windows. Dreams won't go away even after waking. The writer's life, which was supposed to protect against disease, loss, and grief, opens the gates to the enemy.

BUT, YOU ASK, what about the good images? What about the image of the little girl in a field of flowers playing with a puppy that doesn't have the mushroom cloud rising in the background? What about images of the divine, not the demonic? Don't even images with a demonic quality also have a divine quality that makes it hard to live without them?

You live those questions every time you get an image stuck in your head that starts to generate a story or a poem or an essay. But it's not for nothing that the Judeo-Christian-Islamic tradition forbids us to worship the image. It will compete with God—and win, at least in the arena of the human heart.

The terrorists espousing a religion that bans the human image have given themselves and us the burned-into-the-frontal-lobes vision of people jumping from the burning World Trade Center towers. It suggests that behind all human endeavor stands the image, and no matter how we try to suppress it for reasons divine or reasons demonic, the image will find its way into our world.

LET'S PLAY with another image, one that's supposed to be a little more benign.

If you go to the Museum Mares in Barcelona, you will find a collection of carved wooden figures of the crucified Christ. They range in age from four hundred to a thousand years. The crosses they were attached to have crumbled with the churches that held them.

There are fifty or so of them, hanging on the bare walls of the museum, but their cumulative effect is one of incalculable suffering rendered in loving and patient detail. In spite of the centuries they span, you can imagine them as the product of a single obsessed artist. All bear the marks of the scourge, the lacerations of the crown of thorns, the bent shoulders that carried the cross to Calvary, and streaming blood turned black with age. The spear wound is under each right breast, a bleeding hole that shows no ghost occupies the premises. What is left is human husk, broken and battered.

When I flew out of Boise, Idaho, to visit Barcelona a few years ago, the Boise media were caught up with a political controversy about a huge blue neon cross that has stood on a tableland above Boise since the 1950s. When civil libertarians pointed out the cross stood on State of Idaho land and thereby violated the separation of church and state, state and local officials arranged a quick and legally suspect land transfer to the Boise Jaycees, who had put up the cross in the first place.

I made an easy judgment about the matter: if you're going

to put up a giant neon sign for a religion that says you shouldn't steal, you probably shouldn't acquire the land it's on in a back-door public land swindle.

However, in the Museum Mares the Christ images began to unravel my comfortable conclusion about the neon cross. It came to me that Christianity is far more than an attractive bargain made with God where you can follow a few simple rules and in return, gain eternal life. It's a religion that has at its deep center death by torture and unbearable loss. Its focus is not on the next world but on what is missing in this one. The artists who rendered the body of Christ were not focused on resurrection. Instead, they were intent on representing dead flesh at its deadest.

Their literal message—that little is left after the god is gone—is negatively but powerfully evocative of the divine, so much so that it occurred to me that Christianity in Europe a thousand years ago and the civic religion represented by Boise's cross have little in common. But a thousand years is plenty of time to get off message. All Moses had to do was go for a short hike and his people started worshipping a golden calf.

When you remove Christ from the cross and turn it into a giant nightlight, you're making radical changes in what and why you worship. Pastors in Boise churches promise light and eternity and heaven without much thought given to their drawbacks. At Boise churches, they don't talk about the light so great it blinds, the immortal Sibyl who prays for death, and the failure of artists like Dante or Bosch or Milton to invent heavens anywhere near as interesting as their hells. In fact, you'll likely hear that life in heaven is a lot like an endless summer in the mountains of Idaho, but without the tourists. The light has been reduced to a weak and comforting glow, one that protects against the dark but doesn't interfere with sleep.

So it's fair to note that the neon cross above Boise could be, without modification, an advertisement for a medical insurance company. Believe in our program and you won't have to die, is the message, and that is pretty much what they will tell you upon your being admitted to a cancer or cardiac ward. The buildings in Boise most like the great Catalan cathedrals—with similar collections of talismans, relics, high priests, acolytes, and sinners—are Boise's two great hospitals, St. Luke's and St. Alphonsus.

The prayers in Boise hospitals are far more fervent than the ones in Boise churches, and our most sincere hosanna is Thank God I'm Insured. Perdition comes when you can't get on the list for a transplant.

Lost in this vision of things is the enormous reality of death. It has been transformed into an unpleasant but short surgical procedure that delivers you intact to the hereafter.

The Spanish artists who were carving holes in the sides of their Christ-images had a different idea. They showed their god violently involved with mortality. A cross without crucifix numbs us not only to that violence but also numbs us to the stunning idea of a god choosing to become mortal. There's no counterpoint to the desire of mortals to become gods.

But it's no accident that the stock characters in contemporary religious drama are the faithless priest, the priestlike physician, the pious politician, the greedy revivalist, and the born-again hypocrite. It's no accident that you can recognize their powerful spirits even as you search in vain for their souls.

SOUL AND SPIRIT are used interchangeably in the religion of the Blue Cross. But they are opposites of a sort. There are remnants of this opposition in our language, and if you look at their traditional associations you can see it. Image tends toward soul, and word toward spirit. But here are some other associations:

- Spirit is male, soul is female.
- Spirit is sky, soul is earth.
- Spirit: mortification of the flesh. Soul: flesh.
- Spirit: high hopes. Soul: deep dreams.
- Spirit: mind. Soul: heart.
- Spirit: Bach. Soul: Barry White.
- Spirit: neon. Soul: blood.
- Spirit: zeitgeist. Soul: Gethsemane.
- Spirit: health. Soul: suffering.
- Spirit: wealth. Soul: charity.
- Spirit: form. Soul: content.
- Spirit: faith. Soul: mystery.

These are dualities central to our bitterest cultural battles, but they are bound up with one another. They lose meaning in the absence of the other. You can win the battle against soul, only to have the victory lose all meaning.

THIS CULTURE has fled so far in the direction of the spirit that the lives of its people have become empty and airbrushed. Your compensatory task as a writer can be characterized as soul work. So you need to approach the nightmare image, in whatever form it takes: the living, bleeding earth, the flesh in all its decay and fecundity, the delicate beating heart, the messiness of human relationship, your own terrifying inner Barry White, your own lonely inner Gethsemane.

Walk toward any one of those images, begin to throw imperfect words at it, play with the ways that you can turn those words against themselves, and you'll begin to fill a terrible vacuum in the starved souls of the people who read your work.

While you're at it, avoid becoming in any sense the powerful and medically secure male who flies through the sky to make distant business deals, who affects classical music and Jesus-mediated life-extension, who invests in the stock market and real estate, who ignores his feelings, who mortifies his flesh at the gym and has an aversion to all bodily fluids except good clean sweat, and who, when he uses the word love at all, pronounces it as a one-syllable word.

What this poor man—and he exists in all of us who have grown up in this culture, regardless of gender—what this poor man has done is place his faith far in the direction of language and spirit, and empty ritual, and wealth, and sees them all as a way to not think about what his soul might want.

Jesus of Barcelona doesn't inspire respect for any of those things. He does inspire respect for mute suffering, for human life in its absence, and for the sacrament of death. He reminds us that the beginning for Christianity lay in the divine wanting to become mortal flesh and not the human desire to be immortal.

That's where a single image can lead you if you use language as a tool to approach it rather than as a tool to obscure it. Be careful of the images you approach, and even more careful with the words you use to approach them.

SO BACK to Hemingway, who occupies the place of Jesus in the minds of many writers. Usually these writers are male, and haven't entirely laid the issues of adolescence to rest, and what they're attracted to is not Hemingway's writing but Hemingway's image: the adventurer, the lover, and the Death is My Painkiller guy who coolly killed charging water buffalo and got in fistfights with other authors and went to bullfights because he wanted to get to the bare bones of life—the man who scorned the women he couldn't have, who scorned people who didn't lie awake in the dark because they couldn't see the dark, who scorned critics, scorned agents, scorned editors, scorned academics, scorned weakness, and finally scorned his own talent and anything else that he couldn't control. You see where I'm going with this.

In central Idaho we see a lot of twenty-five-year-old guys with little Toyota pickups with kayaks strapped to their shells and backpacks and fly rods and climbing gear inside, and behind the front seat copies of Hemingway's collected stories and *The Sun Also Rises* and *The Old Man and the Sea*. They also have a leather-bound journal or a laptop, because they're writers, or planning on being writers, or think they're writers even though their pages and their hard drives remain blank, or worse, full of self-pity and scorn for the things they once loved and delighted in.

But they're not writers. They have not figured out what it is in their experience that is worth writing about. They're pretending to be writers because Ernest Hemingway created an image that is eating them for breakfast, and its imperatives have become their imperatives. Its face has become their collective face, and it's not a face that will stand up well to the passage of time.

I can say this because when I was twenty-five the only thing that kept me from being one of the young men I describe is that I didn't have a Toyota pickup. If I hadn't escaped that image I never would have become a writer, never would have discovered that the really important work is care and feeding of a soul, or that I had a soul to care for and feed, or that writing is one of the good and strong ways you can do that.

That's as close as I can come to saying that Hemingway's own image destroyed him and it would have destroyed me if I hadn't begun to negotiate with it by twisting and turning and playing with the language in order to come to terms with the terror and love it inspired and the scorn it had for my life. After a while I finally got free of the worst parts of it. That's as close as I can come to dream interpretation.

SCORN MUST HAVE BEEN central to whatever ate Hemingway. I'd guess that if you're headed for suicide, scorn for the things you love will be a big part of you. And it's not a huge leap at this point to say that the image that haunts you enough to generate a story, as terrifying as it is, still contains elements that you love. Love always demands more than you're humanly able to give, and if you think scorn is one way to deal with that situation, you're wrong. Go back to that particular story, tear it apart, and find the moment where you gazed at the image and turned away because you both hated and loved it, and muster up the courage that failed you the first time.

Rules for Writers

Ten Things to Ponder if You're Messing about with Images

1. If depression or grief or bad luck puts you in the Underworld, look around while you're down there. Persephone has
   some nice stuff.

2. The image is by nature pain, and the first impulse of language is to provide comfort and insulation from that pain.
   The second impulse is to reach out to the image and its pain.

3. You learn to reach the image through the active subversion
   of language.

4. If an image that moves you doesn't also frighten you, you're
   not looking at it as closely as you should.

5. Paradox, absurd metaphor, surgery without anesthesia, the
   slaughter of darlings, irony that approaches nihilism—these
   need to be in your writer's toolkit.

6. Destruction and creation coexist simultaneously and uneas-
   ily in writing. It's easy to say that you need to be a writer first
   and then put on another hat and become your own editor,
   but it doesn't work that way.

7. If you're lucky, the writer and the editor in you will accept the
   principle of mutually assured destruction and learn to put up
   with each other. The best I can say for this arrangement is
   that sometimes the editor saves the writer from going down

the wrong path, and the writer saves the editor from reducing the story to a rehash of proven and predictable technique.

8. If you go too far with the destruction of language in order to get close to the image, the image will eat you. Think again of the image of the drowned Hemingway. Without words, it has the power to become witness to its own witness—in a horribly real sense, to trade places with the dreamer. But with a narrative to go along with it, a riverbank to walk and a crowd to talk to, a spring flood and a bridge, it becomes possible to live and laugh in its presence.

9. Keep a list of the images that have awakened your soul. It's your personal iconography.

10. There are words that make it possible to live in this world, dark comic fictions that make it possible to heal and to laugh.

8

Writing Depth

I found myself at the edge of a cosmic abyss.

—Carl Jung

MY UNCLE, Grant Rember, was an expert fly fisherman who fished in Idaho's world-renowned Silver Creek for most of his life. He was not a catch-and-release guy. He killed every fish he caught. He took his catch home to Hailey and gave it to the old poor people around town. He had a small pickup with a snowplow and he plowed driveways and shoveled walks for the same people in the winter. He kept a lot of people living in their own homes longer than they could have otherwise with the addition of fish and the removal of snow.

Twenty years ago, Silver Creek became catch-and-release only. Grant began fishing in the Richfield Canal, further south. The canal was hard to fish, but he mostly came home with his limit. But by then some of the old people were dead and most of the rest of them were being forced out of Hailey as the town became an upscale ghetto. Grant kept fishing in the face of these changes, refining his art until, as he said himself, he was the best fisherman in the county. I don't doubt that he was—he had spent forty years at it, fishing every day he wasn't working, learning as much as he could each time he went. Other fishermen would have been a lot better if Grant hadn't seen fish as food, which was one of the reasons he despised the fly fishermen who went to Silver Creek. It became Grant's joke that fish in Silver Creek had been caught and released so many times that when hooked they would swim to the net and hold their mouth open so the hook could be removed. If you weren't quick about it they would tell you to hurry up.

At the same time Silver Creek became catch-and-release, one of the local newspapers asked Jack Hemingway, Ernest's son, to write a column on fly fishing.

One of Jack Hemingway's columns was about the beauty of catch-and-release fly fishing on Silver Creek, and toward the end of it he made the mistake of saying that he wished he could catch and release the quail and pheasant he shot while bird hunting. Grant read this column and mentioned to me in passing that he thought Jack Hemingway was an idiot. "Why doesn't he shoot blanks?" my uncle asked me.

In this conversation I told my uncle that Jack's nickname, given to him by his father, had been Bumby.

A few years later I was introduced to Jack Hemingway at a party. He looked at me and said, "You're not any relation to *Grant* Rember, are you?"

"He's my uncle," I said. Jack Hemingway moved away slowly and started talking to somebody else.

A few years after that I found out my uncle had started stalking Jack Hemingway after the quail shooting column, walking up to him in the local tackle shops and shouting, "Hey Bumby!

Why don't you just shoot blanks, Bumby?" Then he would criticize Bumby's latest column, Bumby's skills as a fisherman, Bumby's manhood and Bumby's financial insulation from the real world and real work, and finally Bumby's father who had given him that awful name.

Jack Hemingway stopped writing the column about the time his daughter Margaux died. He himself died a couple of years later, losing out in the competition he had with his siblings to see how long a Hemingway could live. My Uncle Grant outlasted him also, and took satisfaction in that.

But it's *Ernest* Hemingway who seems powerful in this story—powerful enough to overshadow the free movement of Grant Rember and Jack Hemingway, and powerful enough to deliver the modeling contract that Jack's daughter Margaux got that gave her a million dollars at an age when her preoccupations were not about saving her money and living a quiet life.

Grant never read Ernest Hemingway's "Big Two-Hearted River," but if he had, he would have understood that story's insistence that even though the river can drown you, you keep fishing. You're after something more important than the experience of fishing—you're after something that dwarfs your experience and yet is separate from your experience.

Our scientific-material culture tells us that if something cannot be experienced, it doesn't exist. I'm hoping to convince you otherwise—that all knowledge is not empirical knowledge, that there is a *gnosis*, a knowledge that exists in opposition to experience.

In fishing, it's known as The Big One That Got Away. For fishermen, it's more real than anything else. I'm hoping to show you something similar exists for writers as well.

Grant would have understood that "Big Two-Hearted River" is about *gnosis* but never would have used the word. Instead, he would have said the story was repetitious and simple-minded and composed of steer manure, and then he would have criticized Hemingway's camping technique. Then he would have declared Ernest Hemingway a phony, which was something he did anyway without ever having read a page of Hemingway's writing.

There was always a large gap between what my Uncle Grant knew and what he had experienced.

In the face of these things I remember Grant's words: "Hey, Bumby! Why don't you just shoot blanks, Bumby? Bumby, listen to me!"

GO DEEPER is terrifying to hear if you're in the middle of a life-and-death struggle to birth a story. When you're staring directly into the gap between what you know and what you cannot say or don't want to say or don't know enough to say, the last thing you want to hear is Go Deeper.

Go Deeper is maddening to hear if you've just finished a final draft, because chances are that you think you've gone deeper already, and worse yet, someone seems to be seeing a direction in your work you can't see yourself.

You may feel like a Bumby in those moments, hounded by a curmudgeon who took your nice sentiment about keeping little birds alive and happy and only saw a cowardly evasion of all the blood and broken feathers of life. Writing is not a catch-and-release sport, is what you're being told, mostly when you haven't realized you've released anything and sometimes when you haven't even realized you've caught anything.

It's not a happy writing moment to be told to go deeper. Going deeper is not an unequivocally good thing anyway. Here's how Hemingway must have experienced it, writing as Nick Adams in "Big Two-Hearted River:"

> He did not feel like going on into the swamp...He felt a reaction against deep wading with the water deepening up under his armpits, to hook big trout in places impossible to land them. In the swamp the banks were bare, the big cedars came together overhead, the sun did not come through, except in patches; in the fast deep water, in the half-light, the fishing would be tragic...Nick did not want it. He did not want to go down the stream any further today.

This is not fishing that Hemingway is talking about here. It's drowning. The story ends with the prophetic statement: "There were plenty of days coming when he could fish the swamp." Hemingway, though, eventually got around to hunting the swamp.

WHEN SOMEONE says, "Go deeper," it may be a good idea, if you're a writer, to send your characters down there ahead of you and see how they do.

Faulkner tried that with Quentin Compson in *The Sound and the Fury*. Faulkner was no stranger to the weight of Southern history, and to psychological impotence, and to loving someone who couldn't love back, but he sent Quentin ahead to check those things out. When Quentin didn't return, Faulkner backed up a bit in time, pulled Quentin out of the water, and used Quentin's condemned voice to speak the long monologue

Absalom, Absalom!—which will hold the place for the Great American Novel until you or I write it.

Sending just your characters into the deep has an unexpected benefit: sometimes they come up from the depths clutching whole books in their dead arms. But the relationship between writer and character is such that if you send a character in your place, he may return unannounced to your door, push it open, and wrap his drowned river-bottom self around you in a muddy embrace.

HERMAN MELVILLE also serves as a cautionary figure here. In *Moby Dick*, Melville's Captain Ahab hates his great totem— the whale—so much that he wants to kill it and drag it wholly into the human world. Instead, the whale drags Ahab into its world. But before that happens, Melville dives deep into Ahab.

Melville said that with *Moby Dick*, he had written a terribly wicked book. Where that wickedness lay for Melville was in his own willingness to know Ahab like a brother, and to participate in Ahab's need for revenge, his rage, his pride, his willingness to sacrifice others to his cause, his ability to defy God, and finally, his love of death. Ahab's virtues are the virtues of the damned. I don't think you can create a character that virtuous and live with him for the couple of years it takes to write a book without those virtues becoming your own.

Melville did not back up in time and pull Ahab out of the water for another book. Instead, after *Moby Dick*, he pulled away from depth. Two years after *Moby Dick* he wrote "Bartelby the Scrivener," whose enduring line is, "I would prefer not to." It's maddening to read "Bartelby," because of Bartelby's refusal to do anything but refuse.

It's maddening to read any of Melville's post-*Moby Dick* works, because of Melville's refusal to approach the depths that he reached with Ahab. Instead he turned more and more toward Christian salvation and epic poetry, which might have been good for him as a person, but it wasn't good for him as a writer. Melville's short novel *Billy Budd* approaches the level of horror of *Moby Dick,* but is about a man who is innocent before God and condemned by men, rather than about a man who is guilty in God's eyes, utterly doomed, and unrepentant about it. Melville lost his taste for defying God.

Joseph Conrad picked up the thread where Melville had dropped it, and because he did we have *Heart of Darkness* and *The Secret Sharer.*

It may be that Melville felt he had to choose between the virtues of God and the virtues of Satan, but that's not a choice a writer should have to make. Writers should be able to claim any virtues they can, no matter who they come from.

FOR SOME TIME NOW I've been interested in *The Book of Job*. It's a story of pain and guilt and trickery and innocence. I've written about pain and guilt and trickery, and I thought maybe if I paid attention to Job, I could write some day about innocence.

But I'm most intrigued by *The Book of Job* because it's the autobiography of a writer. It's a memoir, and memoir writers never have uncomplicated relationships with God.

Need evidence? Listen to the man whine:

> My servants refuse to hear me
> They shun me like a leper

My breath sickens my wife
My stench disgusts my brothers

Even young children fear me
When they see me, they run away
My dearest friends despise me
I have lost everyone I love
Have pity on me, my friends,
For God's fist has struck me.

Then he says:

If only my cry was recorded
And my plea written in a book,
Carved with an iron stylus
Chiseled in rock forever
Someday my witness would come.

This passage is not Job prophesying that Christ is coming, as a lot of Christian theologians have asserted. Instead, it is the self-indulgent voice of memoir. Job's eloquent complaints, his self-pity, his insistence on his own innocence, his belief in the power of words—all these argue that at least some of Job's torments had to do with his wanting to be a writer.

THE BOOK OF JOB is a four-part poem framed by a prose prologue and a prose epilogue. Briefly, the story begins when God's literary agent shows up at God's doorstep and God asks him what he's been doing. Satan says he's been wandering the earth, looking things over, trolling for manuscripts to sit on. God asks

Satan if he's seen his most excellent servant Job, and Satan says, in effect, Job wouldn't be so excellent if you weren't encouraging him to think he has talent.

God takes Satan's words as a challenge and tells Satan that he can take away all of Job's wealth and his family and his herds. Satan does so. Job's response is "The Lord Giveth, The Lord Taketh Away, Praised be the Lord."

God suggests that such praise is proof that Job is his true and faithful servant.

Satan says maybe so, but that as long as Job is walking around, healthy, it doesn't cost him anything to mouth praises.

God gets tired of this argument. "Whatever," he says. "Do your damnedest."

So Satan gives Job the mange, and boils, and terrible body odor, and as the poetry part of Job's story starts, he's sitting in a pile of excrement, scratching scabs with a broken piece of a pot, in a clinical depression.

THE FIRST THREE PARTS of the poem take the form of a criminal trial. Job is visited by three friends, who in three increasingly intense rounds of speeches, insist that Job's misfortunes are Job's fault. God is just, they say. God plays by the rules. They quote Einstein and tell Job that God does not play dice with the universe. Job must have sinned and just not realized it.

After each speech by each of his friends, Job says he's innocent. He complains ever more loudly. By the third round of speeches, Job's friends are calling him an out-and-out sinner and he's telling them whatever claim they had on his friendship is gone. He tells them God is God and he can do what he wants, but he, Job, deserves better. Then Job finally does something that should doom him. He calls God out.

"You got a problem with me?" he says to God. "Spit it out. Because I'm not getting it. Whatever you think I did, I didn't."

So far *The Book of Job* looks like the trial of Job. But something ironic and literary is happening here. We readers already know that God and Satan have cooked up this situation together. We know that it's God who is unjust and capricious. God has sinned against Job and hasn't realized it. So the trial of Job reverses to the trial of God.

If *The Book of Job* is the autobiography of a writer, the writer is getting into pretty deep trouble right now.

The fourth section of the poem is God's defense. Even if Job's friends don't understand that God is the accused here, God does, and he speaks out of a whirlwind and acts as his own aggrieved attorney. He's also the judge, jury, and witness.

"Who is this whose ignorant words cover my design with darkness?" says God. "Listen and I will speak; I will question you. Please instruct me." This is divine sarcasm. You don't ask for instruction when you're omniscient. Job doesn't say anything in return, which is smart.

> "Where were you when I planned the earth?" God asks.
> "Have you walked through the depths of the ocean
> Or dived to the floor of the sea?
> Have you stood at the gates of doom
> Or looked through the gates of death?
> Have you seen the edge of the universe?
> Speak up, if you have such knowledge."

Job can't answer, and God asks a lot more questions. In those questions, God evokes the glory of creation. He also delivers to Job a pure knowledge of the cosmos, and the words of the poem show Job's failing struggle to bridge the gap between what he has come to know in the depths of his heart and what he can express.

At the moment that Job is trying to somehow encompass all this unencompassable knowledge, God asks Job why he is silent.

Job says he's maybe said too much already. There's being right and there's being dead, is what Job is thinking, and right now they're looking pretty similar.

Job is also realizing that maybe the universe isn't human-centered. Maybe God has other concerns than Job's servants and flocks and general prosperity.

At this point, the story drives the point home with image. The supreme strength—even the *divine* strength—of images is that they can't be argued with.

God shows Job Behemoth, a gigantic bull-like beast God has created as a toy, one with bones of iron, a tree-like penis, and testicles churning with seed.

God then explains that there are creatures in the sea too big to fish for. He tells Job that hope—if Job still has any at this point—is false hope, and gives Job a vision of Leviathan, a great amphibious beast with horrible curving teeth, a skin armored with spikes, glowing eyes, smoking nostrils, flaming breath, and an enormous beating heart. Chariots will disappear between those teeth. Arrows will bounce off those scales.

Leviathan is the Big One, the crown of creation, and his power and his inhuman majesty are too much for Job. Job starts talking to God again, even though he has said he won't.

Job acknowledges that God can do anything he wants, but Job won't quit while he's ahead, which is another reason I think Job is a writer.

Instead, in what is possibly the most ironic passage in the Bible, Job quotes God's words back to him and asks the crucial question of this story: *"Who is this whose ignorant words cover my design with darkness?"*

If not for the prose prologue, these words wouldn't make sense, but because of the prologue we can see the irony. God has been covering his own design with darkness. He's been fooling himself, something he tends to do whenever Satan comes around. These words also hint that language can obscure what is real. Used carelessly, it creates a distance from creation.

Job, finally and literally coming to his senses, says:

> "I have heard you with my ears; but now my eyes have seen you. Therefore I will be quiet, comforted that I am dust."

Even in this moment Job lets the reader know that the relationship between Job and God remains that of questioner and questioned. There's been a change in the cosmic order. From here on out, in the evolution of human consciousness, visions can be demanded of God.

Job's last words in the story indicate something else has occurred. Job is dust all right, but he's conscious dust, dust with a sense of irony, dust possessed of understanding, dust that demands justice, dust that dares to continue to interrogate God. That definition of dust is also a pretty good definition of what it means to be a writer who dares to go deeper.

In the prose epilogue, God rebukes Job's three friends for not seeing the true nature of Himself and demands they sacrifice seven bulls and seven rams to make things right with him. God restores Job's wealth and gives him new flocks and new sons and daughters, and "there were no women as beautiful as Job's daughters. He gave them a share of his possessions along with their brothers." In a story obsessed with justice, Job's conscious choice to impose gender equity is the first instance of it. In the end, it's Job, tempered by suffering, who brings justice into his own story.

CARL JUNG, in his monograph *Answer to Job*, saw Job's story as a parable of humanity forced to consciousness by a god unable to recognize his own dark side. Because Jung saw supernatural phenomena as manifestations of the psyche, the story becomes a psychological journey, a coming together of disparate elements of the mind. It is a way in which the ego's questioning and complaint and whining and outrage can force humans to become aware of the whole of who they are. Become aware of that whole, Jung said, and you'll recognize that God lies within you and not outside of you. Jung calls that part of the self the God Image.

To put it in terms useful to writers, the story of Job is the story of the writer who writes to become aware of the universe as it is, to make conscious what is not conscious, to make whole what is not whole. Writing on some level is sin, because it places us in conflict with a God who cannot bear to have us understand him better than he understands himself.

AS WE KNOW from reading Jonathan Edwards and Cotton

Mather and Dante, sin causes pain. Some of that pain will come from following all the rules and still getting your work rejected by your agent.

"I think this needs to be a little deeper," she'll say. "Frankly, I'm not sure I can sell this."

And then you go back to your downward psychological journey, trying to figure out new rules while staring at a blank screen and being visited by internal buddies. They look just like the kids your parents wouldn't let you hang out with when you were in high school. They tell you, "You must be doing something wrong or this would be easier." Or "All you have to do is set up a regular writing schedule and that novel will just finish itself." They will tell you your writing is good but not important. Then they'll drag you out to go drinking. The part of yourself that you'd really like to have visit you—the God who is willing to show you his power—will remain as silent and as distant as Andromeda.

This sort of thing can go on longer and create more pain than you think you can bear. But keep going back to it, keep trying to close the gap between what you know and what you can express, keep trying to dive into what Thomas Pynchon has called the "concealed density of dream," and at some point you'll find yourself whining and complaining and wishing you had never been born and muttering under your breath about whoever has set things up so that you spend your life staring into a blank screen. Go deep enough into your own pain, nurture your self-pity as if it were a hothouse orchid, frame your problems as the world's problems long enough and you'll begin to make your own ego the most important thing in the universe.

That's when God will get angry, because you're on his turf.

You'll start to hear the sound of a whirlwind.

At this point, it's not important whether he's inside or outside, God or God Image. You're in for some divinely-delivered knowledge, whether you want it or not.

If you're lucky the way Job was lucky, you won't die. Instead, God will tell you that you are less than nothing compared to his creation, and that any hope you had of making a mark on the universe is a lie.

"Hope is a lie?" you'll ask. "Why?"

It's the Cindy Lou Who moment in every writer's life.

If your luck holds, you will come away knowing things impossible to know. It will destroy any idea that you're in control of your writing, but it will give you a consciousness of how ridiculous and small humans are in the face of the cosmos, how futile their greatest efforts.

After you've had time to digest the insignificance of the person you call "I," you will understand how much there is to write about. It will open you to a great and serendipitous vision.

Close your eyes and that vision will remain, inscribed on your eyelids. It will demand that you throw words at it, that you babble in the face of it, and that you keep trying even though you'll never be able to get as close as you need to get to it. Like the Big One that my uncle tried to catch for forty years, it is always just out of your depth. But you can come close, and spend your life getting closer with every failure, which may be what a state of grace looks like for the writer.

If a cosmic vision is a bit too mystical for you, you can take comfort in the fact that the same words could be used to describe a psychotic break.

LET'S GO BACK to my Uncle Grant for a moment.

Grant gave me fly-fishing lessons until I was twelve. At that point I started asking too many questions. For a while he tried to show me rather than tell me the answers to questions, but when things got too verbal he quit taking me fishing, which is why my fly-fishing skills remain at the junior-high level.

He would have been impatient if I had ever said I would write about fishing. "If you're going to write," he would have said, "Write. If you're going to fish, fish. Don't conflate the two."

I probably would have asked him what I was supposed to write about.

"I don't know," he would have said. "But something besides fishing."

"But fishing," I would have said, "is a rich source of metaphors. Water itself can be seen as a way of evoking psychological depth."

"If you're going to write about psychological depth," he would have said, "Write about psychological depth. Leave the water out of it."

We never had that conversation, but we must have had similar ones, because when I think about the people who taught me to write, Grant is one of them. In my own writing, I try to articulate his directness, his plain speaking, his clear vision, his honesty, his compulsive de-mystification of things, his continual attempt to get better at anything he did, his mistrust of authority, and his absolute hatred of phoniness, lying, secretiveness and ambiguity.

So Leviathan is not a metaphor. It's just Leviathan, the death of hope, and the death of hope is not a metaphor either. Behemoth's penis really is the size of a pine tree, and his testicles really are churning with seed, and he has no need of Viagra.

When Melville looks into the blank white mirror of the whale's forehead, he really does see the void in the center of a hating human being, and it is a real void and real hate. Ahab does not die because he meets a giant white metaphor, he dies because acting on his hate has resulted in his being lashed to an animal that is better at holding its breath under water than he is. The Big Two-Hearted River really will drown you if you go over the big blown-down cedar and into the swamp where you couldn't land a fish anyway because it would twist the line around washed-out tree roots. The burden of Southern history will not kill you, but the ordinary people who inscribe its myths and taboos upon you will. Hemingway and Faulkner and Melville and God, raging at Job, have just one message: this stuff is real.

MAYBE THIS IS a good point to say there are women writers who have risked as much and suffered as much and got as deep as the male writers I've mentioned. What happened to them in the larger culture brings up issues that should be explored in another book, preferably one not written by an aging white male.

But here is a thought experiment in the form of a sculpture: Edwina Sandy's *Christa*, which shows a female Christ, breasts bare and drooping, crowned with thorns and nailed to a cross. Sandy's sculpture throws a glimmer of light on the fact that our cultural reality has pushed female suffering into a different and less accessible place than male suffering.

Working with the shock of recognition is always dangerous work for an artist, which is why most of us try to stick with the shock of the new.

SO GOING DEEPER means understanding that the deep is all around you, it's not just beneath your feet. Think of looking through a telescope deep into space. It's a condition of where you are and not a direction you're pointed at.

It involves seeing that the metaphor you can't wait to get into your writing is usually an evasion of the hard work of putting the truth into words. It involves leaving what you expected to write on the cutting room floor. It involves the courage to challenge the unjust way the world is put together, and the realization that if anybody is going to be self-conscious and honest and courageous around here, it's going to be you. That's why the usual unseen companion line to Go Deeper is, "You go deeper. I'll wait here for the cops."

It's not that experienced writers have learned cowardice, although writing careers have ended because of a failure of nerve, when they haven't ended with the awarding of tenure.

Most working writers *have* learned caution, and know there are depths they don't want to plumb *yet*. The "yet" is evidence that they're still alive as writers.

When you look at Go Deeper that way, it's easier to see that the journey you're being urged to begin is yours alone. Sometimes writing advisors have ambitions for how deep our students will go, but we also know those ambitions are secondary to what our students discover once they're down there, looking around.

ERNEST BECKER'S *The Denial of Death* serves as a companion volume to *The Book of Job*. Becker's thesis is that the idea of death tears our minds in half. Like Job before the whirlwind, we know what it means to be mortal and puny and irredeemably small and yet exquisitely aware of the beauty and majesty and infinite scope of the cosmos.

Becker says that's the human condition—that sooner or later, if we live long enough, the torments of Job come upon us—and Becker says we run from that knowledge by shopping 'til we drop, or getting face-down-in-the-gutter drunk, or using drugs, or getting religion or politics, or screwing ourselves silly, or engaging in litigation, or working at a career, or abusing our spouses, or becoming military heroes, or going back to school for yet one more degree.

All are evasions of the truth of our lives, and Becker treats them all with more or less the same contempt.

But here's the happy part: the one thing we do that Becker does not treat with contempt is our art. When we are writing or painting or fishing at the level of intensity my Uncle Grant brought to fishing, we are single-mindedly creating a world, and for a moment, the energy we spend trying not to think about our death is free to serve the cause of creation.

Becker says those moments are the closest we can come to being godlike. When he was writing his book, which must have required all his knowledge, imagination, and skill, the fact that he himself was dying from cancer must have seemed like an irrelevancy. The last chapter reads like he was cut off in mid-thought.

I hope we, as writers, go with Becker's courage to see the world as it is and to see how pathetic and small humans are in relation to it. I hope that we can come to understand that our only reply to that world is our tiny, conscious, and sometimes stupidly courageous voices.

Rules for Writers

Uncle Grant's Ten Tips for Writers Who Think Writing is Like Fishing

1. If you think fishing is a metaphor, you're going to be eating mac and cheese for dinner.

2. The truth is hard to put into words. Don't make it harder by using tropes.

3. If your standards are high enough, you'll still be learning how to fish forty years from now.

4. Don't limit what you know to what you've experienced.

5. Luck is involved any time you go fishing. But if you don't know how to fish, you won't have any luck.

6. The Big One is down there.

7. It's better to have the Big One on your line than a bunch of little ones in your creel.

8. Don't wade in over your boots unless you don't mind getting wet.

9. Be generous with what you catch.

10. If you have a kid, don't call him Bumby.

9

Writing Mom

Had we not better glance through the main facts in our own lives—
not in our individual careers but in our make-up as human beings?
—E.M. Forster

I HAD DONE everything possible to avoid writing. I had written letters, made myself a cup of tea, addressed Christmas cards, fed the dog, cleaned up my email inbox, and shoveled snow off the deck. I had run out of excuses, and was finally getting down to addressing the issue of writing about my mother—when she called.

"This is Betty Rember," she said. "Who is this?"

"Your son, John," I said.

"Did you call?" she asked.

My mother was ninety years old and had Alzheimer's. She was in an assisted living facility three hours away by car. When she called me, even if she forgot she was calling, it meant she was up to the complex task of finding my number on the notepad beside her bed, dialing it, and waiting for the response. When she called it was by definition one of her good days. The only time it wasn't good for her to have a good day was when it was three o'clock in the morning and she was in a panic because she didn't know where she was.

"No," I said. "You called me. What's on your mind?"

"I was wondering where your father was," she said.

"Gone," I said.

"Gone where?"

"Mom, Dad died six years ago."

"He did? I thought he put me in here and got married to someone else."

"That was me, Mom. Dad died in 2001. You lived at the ranch for five years before we had to put you in assisted living. He loved you very much all of his life. He died loving you."

"My memory," she began, "is shot. Have my parents gone back to Iowa?"

"They died too."

"When?"

"Your mother died in 1952. Your father died in 1964."

"I don't know where I am in time," she said. This bit of self-consciousness meant she was having a very good day.

"You're ninety years old, Mom. You've earned the right to jump around a bit on the calendar."

She laughed. Then she said she liked where she was because she was treated well there and she knew she couldn't live alone, which meant she was having an incredibly good day. I told her about the weather—it was a cold blue-sky day—and that I was going to go skiing if I got some writing done.

"You're not skiing by yourself, are you? Please don't go skiing by yourself." Like so many of the things my mother said those days, it was a reflex, not a sentence.

Two hours later, I found myself skiing alone down the hill behind my house, angry, taking chances with thin snow and rusty skills and fifty-nine-year-old bones, skiing fast between deadfall and rocks, telling myself that Jesus Christ I'm Old Enough To Ski By Myself Mom, which really doesn't qualify as telling yourself anything. Julie was in Boise and wouldn't be back for a couple of days, and if something went wrong I would have frozen to death by midnight. I was pretty sure my mother had forgotten what skiing is.

So how did a ninety-year-old woman losing her mind in an assisted living facility still have the power to send me screaming out the door in an adolescent rage, lunging against the knowledge that I'm not an independent being, that I'm someone who can't take the smallest chances with his own life because his purpose in life is to be a bulwark against his mother's grief? Where does that power come from and why won't it go away?

It's like asking where the weather comes from. The weather can kill people—it happens all the time—but we don't call it evil. Laws are not passed against grief, although a lot of laws are passed to keep grief at bay, and a lot of ritual behavior gets started to keep grief at bay, and a lot of people are conceived to keep grief at bay.

Hence me. I am not exaggerating about being a bulwark against my mother's grief. My mother lost a two-year-old son in a household accident in 1946, and over the next five years had four miscarriages and then me. I am here because she was desperately trying to replace the child she lost and was willing to face increasingly worse odds against delivering a healthy baby.

My mother has been a stumbling block for me and for my

writing. I made this discovery when I was talking to my editor at Pantheon about my memoir, *Traplines*. I had written a chapter on my father and my editor had liked it. He gently asked me to write a chapter on my mother. My reaction was quick.

"I'll write about her when she's *dead*," I shouted into the phone, and at that moment a relationship I had spent much of my life setting up—that of writer to editor—became much cooler. Editors for major publishers expect writers to respect their gentle requests, and my editor was no exception.

My mother has since died, and I have begun, with much hesitation and tentativeness, to write about Mom. It's painful for me to do, and if it were painful for just me it probably wouldn't be worth a chapter in this book. But lots of people have Mom trouble.

Possibly it's because your Mom, at a basic physiological level, donated your nutrients during the nine months or so you occupied her body. Probably it's because nurturing and caring for you required that she put aside her own dreams for twenty years and maybe forever. Possibly you and your siblings ate up her life before she had a chance to live it. Possibly her ambitions got passed on to you as the only way they could ever be realized. You may be her way of making a difference in the world, which makes you wonder when you're sitting down to write a story or a novel or a memoir, whose story or novel or memoir it is. The dedication "for my mother and father" that is in so many first published works might well read, "by my mother."

Your mother will see your book as a monument to blood and tears long before your father will. She'll have a handy metaphor for the struggle and pain that it takes to birth a book.

Of course, she may not see your struggle as being akin in any way to her own. My mother took a look at my story collection *Cheerleaders from Gomorrah* when it came out and said, "I don't know where he gets those ideas. Certainly not from me."

But I don't know. Almost every character in that book starts out damned to misery and failure but struggles through to find grace in a form that is neither expected nor desired. That describes my mother's life from the time she lost one child to when she gained its replacement. That's probably as far as I should go as a psychoanalytic critic of my own work.

I'M GOING TO TAKE a leap here, and start talking about the unconscious, which, as you know, can't really be talked about because it's unconscious. You have to use metaphor to talk about it, and metaphors are inaccuracies at best, misleading lies at worst. But I'll ask you to take on faith that the unconscious exists, and that it has a structure, and that we can make inferences about that structure in a manner analogous to a particle physicist making inferences about the subatomic world by studying the tracks in a cloud chamber.

I should warn you that when you talk about the unconscious the metaphors breed like bunnies, and when you're dealing with metaphors you have to remember that they're leg-hold traps for the literal minded. So let's not be literal minded around metaphors unless we want to be confronted with the image of a bunny in a leg-hold trap—his basket of eggs spilled out and broken on the ground.

Carl Jung's essay, *The Spirit of Man in Art and Literature*, suggests that artists, writers among them, stand on the threshold between consciousness and the unconscious. Writers turn to face the unconscious, which leaks screams and the odor of decay and the occasional out-from-under-the-bed abomination and horror. We stare into its darkness until we see a dark shape and we try to find the courage to grasp it—often as not barehanded—and turn it into something conscious and beautiful and articulate. Sometimes, if we're lucky, that shape will be too big for its doorway and will come only halfway through, and even though it smells of brimstone and its words remain bloody and mute, it will deliver enormous energy until a collection of stories have pulled it all the way through to this world.

"Sometimes the story that inspires the book will not make it into the book," is the way I express this idea to the writers I work with.

Another way to put it is that writers spin molten gold into straw. It's a logistically difficult process.

Jung says this process of approaching the unconscious and dealing with its material is hard on artists and sometimes makes their mental states indistinguishable from psychoses. But later in his career he began to suggest that people who refuse to face the unconscious also fall into a psychosis, the psychosis of normalcy, which in twenty-first century America is about the worst craziness around. So when I think of the myth of the artist, I don't think of Pygmalion or Daedalus and his Labyrinth, I think of Jason steering the Argo between Scylla and Charybdis. If you think taking in a Damien Hirst exhibition is dangerous, try buying into consensus reality.

Jung envisioned human development as a process of individuation and soul-building and increasing awareness, and he wrote extensively about the process. What he didn't write much about was the return, in extreme old age, back into the matrix of the unconscious. But that return is a part of human life too, and if you are a writer, it bears closer examination.

On her bad days, my mother's Alzheimer's peeled away her conscious mind and what was often left was a great fear of being abandoned to the forces of grief. She talked of the people who left her as though they did so by choice: the son she lost, her husband, her parents, an older sister who died of a brain tumor when she was nineteen. I learned bad things about people of whom I had always heard good. We spent time looking through old photographs, and the people in them became more real to her than Julie and I, sitting with her in her room in the assisted living facility. Sometimes she seemed to leave us and go into the photographs, and they appeared to have for her the immediacy and vast scope and action of dream.

Once, when looking for a friend of my mother's who lived in the independent living part of the facility, I wandered into the Alzheimer's ward. There, walking along a hallway, hearing the constant blare of alarms when people tried to leave their beds, looking to my left and to my right to see patients, two to a room, staring emptily at TVs, I came face to face with an ancient woman in a wheelchair. Her mouth was open, toothless, and dark, and her eyes unseeing. She was clutching a large stuffed doll, a canvas cylinder with painted-on blue eyes and red mouth and black hair. She was hugging it like it was her baby, and it seemed to me as if the person had left the body and all that was left was the clutch. I hurried out of there as quickly as I could find an exit.

It occurred to me that the assisted living complex could be seen as a metaphor for the psyche—the independent living apartments part as consciousness, the Alzheimer's ward as the chaotic and inarticulate and unreachable yet all too real unconscious, and assisted living, where my mother was, as the permeable threshold between the two. It was on that threshold where my mother made the final meanings of her life, a process exemplified but not circumscribed by her ability to move in and out of photos.

It then occurred to me that much of what I do as a writer is to try to approach that same threshold, placing myself deliberately in that same place Alzheimer's placed my mother, where the unconscious is close enough that space and time have no parameters. It's essential for a writer to be able to go out of the world of keyboard and screen and into the world of image, whether image is a photo or a sudden spindrift of snow along a high ridge, or a sunset over the peaks, or the roof of my house seen from the hill above, or Julie, wearing a bright red and yellow stocking cap and her purple coat, walking across the snowy field with our black dog.

I TELL THE WRITERS who work with me to look for ways to approach the unconscious, and when I do, I use the metaphor of the underworld. The metaphor pretends that the writer can really go into the underworld like Persephone or Hercules and not die. Often I'll use the story of Orpheus descending into Hades, searching for and hoping to rescue his dead lover Eurydice. "Go down there," I say, "and find a story and bring it back up to show people. Because it smells, you clean it off.

Because it's mute and helpless, you teach it to walk and talk."

Not everybody likes this metaphor. For one thing, it's not nice to talk about Eurydice like she's a zombie, even though that's what she no doubt was when Orpheus tried to lead her back to sunlight. He looked back at the last moment to see if she was following him out of Hades, and hit by his gaze, she turned away from love and walked back toward death.

Orpheus mourned her until a group of Thracian women figured out he wasn't going to get over it. They were overcome with jealousy and tore him to pieces.

Some writers don't like this metaphor because it asks too much. Nobody can approach the underworld without penalty, and even greater penalties can come when you pick something up down there and carry it home. You are stealing jewels from the crown of Hades.

The great appeal of genre writing—its safety—comes from the fact that you can't approach the underworld from there. You're simply working off the unconscious material that someone else risked life and limb to get. You can't approach the underworld by writing stories to which you already know the ending. You can't approach the underworld by writing about a world where the evil is domesticated and harmless and preordained to fail.

But a lot of writers aren't worried about the dangers of the underworld. What they really object to is the idea that a story or poem or painting already exists in a place where their skills can't reach. They want to see their stories as their creations, not as things that already have their own reality and the ability to use writers to be born into this world. Writers tend to want to be mothers rather than midwives.

This idea might sound a little strange, but we've all been in workshops where a writer's sense of ownership gets in the way of a really good story. "This is *my* story," is always worrisome to hear. It's much nicer to hear, "This story has latched on to me and it won't let go." There's a vast difference in the position of the writer in those two statements, but also a vast difference in the quality and intensity of stories claimed and stories that claim.

AT THIS POINT, including Mom in a discussion of the underworld might seem unfair. After all, most mothers are nice, sunny, even saintly people, so dedicated to the Life Force—to use a phrase from one of George Bernard Shaw's treatises on the subject—that they may not have had time to live for themselves. I can't go to a big box store and see a nineteen-year-old in her final trimester buying a three month supply of disposable diapers and not think that the girl is about to find out that her life doesn't belong to her anymore. It's tempting to look around and say that motherhood hijacks a life for eighteen years or so and that mother-love is a variation of the Stockholm Syndrome. Who among us can say for certain that conception and birth and the raising of children are not, in essence, acts of violence toward the mother's life, and that a mother who achieves her own life in the face of that violence has accomplished an enormous act of will?

We can call mothers saintly but we run into cultural taboos if we start examining why they're saintly.

But it's in the nature of writers to look at the things nobody else wants to look at. And every writer has a mother, and sooner or later we begin to think about the trajectory a woman's life might have taken if she hadn't become a mother and our mother specifically. This is not a comfortable thought experiment, because the place that unlived life went is into the underworld.

Follow this train of thought not much further, and you can see that for writers, one of the portals to the underworld is Mom.

I think of Eugene O'Neill, who in *Mourning Becomes Electra* and *Long Day's Journey Into Night*—astonishing plays that every writer should read—explored the power of the unconscious maternal sensibility. If you could characterize the whole of O'Neill's work in a sentence—you can't, but if you could—it would be that O'Neill places the audience in the position of a helpless infant in the arms of a woman who is highly ambivalent about motherhood and who seeks to enforce her will upon the world by her passive control of other human beings. This sounds monstrous, and any of you who have sat through *Long Day's Journey* know that it is. But O'Neill knew you couldn't keep a good woman down, no matter how repressive and patriarchal the culture.

OR MAYBE NOT. In the fairy tale *Hansel and Gretel* a poor woodcutter and his wife and two children are starving on the edge of a dark forest. The children's mother (only in later bowdlerized versions of the tale is she their stepmother) urges that the children be abandoned in the forest—where "the wild beasts will tear them apart"—so that all will not starve. The woodcutter at first refuses, but is convinced by his wife's nagging.

They abandon Hansel and Gretel—twice, because the children are aware of the plan and Hansel litters their path with shiny stones and they find their way back. The second time he is only able to scatter bread crumbs, which the birds pick up. Hansel and Gretel wander until they are led by a white bird to the bread-and-candy house of a hungry cannibalistic witch, who captures them. She puts Hansel in a cage and feeds him the best foods, while Gretel is forced to be her servant and eats only crab shells. Hansel gains weight on his diet, but when the witch inspects him he holds out a bone that the nearly blind witch thinks is his finger. Finally the witch becomes impatient and fires up the oven, intending to eat both the children, Gretel as hors d'oeuvre and Hansel as main course.

Gretel tricks the witch into the oven and slams the door. She then frees Hansel and the two of them help themselves to the witch's treasure. They seek their way back home, but are stopped by a large river, which they cannot cross. Gretel calls out to a white duck, who takes them across one at a time. The country suddenly looks familiar, and the children find their home and father. Their mother is dead, and the children enter their father's house, flinging jewels about, and they all "live together in utmost joy," which is an improvement on happily ever after.

This tale—not so benign in the first place—becomes less benign after you've been talking about mothers and the unconscious. My synopsis reveals a progression for the children and their father from famine to plenty, effected by the death of the two adult female characters, one of them Mom. An easy parallel can be drawn between the children's hungry mother and the hungry witch.

The tale can be seen as yet another allegory of a journey into and out of the unconscious. Where Orpheus had Hades, Hansel and Gretel have the dark wood. The famine—everyone is hungry in this story—is the famine of the psyche, and the story solves the famine with the murder of the blind and insatiable witch, who is the recognizable essence of the children's mother, transformed toward the animal by her residence in the unconscious.

That Hansel and Gretel outwit the witch and thereby survive her hospitality demonstrates that though they approach the unconscious, they never enter it. They retain their capacity for conscious thought, and are thus able to trick the dull-witted witch and kill her. Theirs is a story of consciousness triumphant.

But it is also a story of murder. The high point of danger in the story is when Gretel pushes the witch into the oven and slams the door, and it's not too much to assume that the oven is the heart of the dark wood, its deepest point. The witch is trapped there and cannot come out, and at the same time the children's mother, whose hunger was so great that she would sacrifice them to it, also dies. Death in the unconscious causes death in the conscious world.

So one interpretation of *Hansel and Gretel* is that joy is achieved at the price of destroying the story's female component, which exists mainly as a boundless hunger, an unrestrained wanting, even in a situation—the house of bread and candy— where hunger and want should not exist.

It's tempting to say that *Hansel and Gretel* is a metaphor for writing, where consciousness pushes itself toward the unconscious, overcomes great danger, and returns to the daylit world with jewels—items of great value that reduce the problems of the story to a happy economic outcome. But the violence of the story suggests that consciousness never triumphs without a price.

I also worry that if it's triumphant, can it be consciousness? Is the story's joy a conscious joy? Is the river that Hansel and Gretel are carried across really their way home, or is it a deeper journey into a bizarre and inhuman materialist ecstasy? After all, they didn't cross the river on the way *to* the witch's house.

NOBODY CROSSED any rivers on the way to June Cleaver's house. In the 1950s sitcom *Leave It To Beaver,* she was the mother in an archetypal American family of four: her husband, Ward, and sons, Wally and Beaver. The premise of the show was that the Beaver, June's youngest son, would get into trouble at the start of every episode and be out of it by the end, usually by being rescued by his mother's love and wisdom, followed by a stern lecture from his father.

June Cleaver vacuumed her house and baked cookies in high heels and a pearl necklace and fashionable dresses. She acted as mother not only to her own sons but also to the neighborhood children, among them Eddie Haskell, an unctuous little weasel who sucks up to the adults and picks on Beaver Cleaver. Eddie is the only character in the show that comes close to being evil, but his is a penny-ante, easily defeated evil.

June Cleaver went from being a sitcom character to a cultural icon. She became the maternal model not just for women but for huge numbers of men of Beaver Cleaver's generation.

She is notable for having no dark side. She was perfectly put together, and in control. She lacked self-doubt and for that matter any internal life, her psyche being completely occupied by the tasks of household management, motherhood, and acting the benefactress to the neighborhood children.

She was portrayed by the actor Barbara Billingsley, who became wealthy in the role but so locked into its one-sided maternal sweetness that she was not cast in another production for twenty years.

Nobody believed in June Cleaver as a real person. Everyone knew she was a work of fiction, but her power was such that she was singled out by 1960s feminists as one of the great oppressing images in women's lives. People could get enraged just talking about her, and not all of them were women struggling against her portrayal of what a woman should be. Some of them were men and women who had been raised by women who had sacrificed themselves on the altar of June Cleaver motherhood.

JUST A SMALL REMINDER here of the Easter Bunny in the leghold trap. Metaphor is a tempting way to articulate the unarticulable, but it almost always reduces and demystifies and makes absurd its object. Story is an improvement on metaphor, especially when it preserves the complexity and mystery of the thing it's about. Turning story into metaphor almost always kills the story. June Cleaver deprived of the thin sitcom storyline becomes a Stepford Wife, and in that movie the story line is only the predictable working out of a wife-as-zombie metaphor.

That's not the direction we want to go as writers, but it's sometimes hard to resist the forces that would have us metaphorize everything. Resist them anyway. It's not too much to say that metaphor kills story. The Athenian citizen who witnessed Sophocles' *Oedipus Rex* experienced catharsis in a way that the American citizen in traditional psychoanalysis, who is learning to see Oedipus as a metaphor, never will. As in so many other intellectual endeavors, the Greeks got there first and claimed the best real estate.

So let's return to story for a bit. In a 1935 photograph of my mother, she is at the old, now destroyed resort of Salt Air, on the shores of the Great Salt Lake. She's in a dark swimsuit, standing on the edge of a swimming pool. Beside her is her friend Bernyce, who is two years older. They are seventeen and nineteen, both beautiful young women, their smiles betraying recent laughter. In the background, sitting on a bench beside the pool, is a distinguished-looking man of forty-five with a moustache, wearing a business suit and a fedora. He looks impossibly overdressed and formal beside them, as if he had been Photoshopped into the picture.

"That's Uncle Dave," my mother said. She was sitting in a chair in her room at the assisted living facility, and I was sitting beside her, and we were looking at a photo album that Julie had put together out of a suitcase of old photos.

"Who's Uncle Dave?" I asked.

"Uncle Dave was Bernyce's great uncle," she said. She smiled. "Uncle Dave had money. And he liked being in the company of young women. He would take us on trips and pay for everything. We went to California with him and to Lake Louise, in Canada."

Sure enough, on the opposite page of the album there was a photo of my mother standing in the gardens of the Lake Louise Grand Hotel, the lake and glacier and mountains behind her.

"He took you on trips?" asked Julie.

"He was a perfect gentleman," said my mother, answering a question in Julie's voice. "He just liked being in the company of young women. He never did anything improper."

My mother stared into the photograph, and Uncle Dave seemed to look back at her. "Except for one thing," she said. "He always wanted to shave our legs for us. Of course, we didn't let him. It was silly."

I looked at my mother. She was seventeen again, and seeing Uncle Dave as she saw him in 1935. I thought of her career as a registered nurse and thought that at some point in her life she must have realized that what Uncle Dave wanted from her and Bernyce was darker and more tragic than silly. But by then she was building bulwarks against grief, and she must have put that realization out of her mind. Sometimes I think that my mother's Alzheimer's was simply what happens when you put anything that causes emotional pain out of your mind. It's the mental equivalent of when your mother tells you not to make that face because it will stick and you'll go through life that way.

"Are my parents gone?" my mother asked, looking up from Uncle Dave. I wondered how she convinced her parents—or how Uncle Dave convinced her parents—to let her go on those cross-country trips with him. I also wondered who Uncle Dave really was. I had recently discovered that Bernyce didn't have a great uncle Dave.

"Your parents are gone," I said.

"And Helen?" That was her sister who died of a brain tumor. I nodded.

"And Ruth?" Her other sister, nine years younger. I nodded again.

"And Craig?" Her husband.

"And Bernyce?"

"She died this fall," I said, but I didn't tell her that she had gone to Bernyce's funeral. It had been difficult for her and when I had talked to her before the funeral she had wanted to know if Bernyce was going to be there, among the mourners.

"Uncle Dave is gone?" she asked, and I thought of Uncle Dave in Hades, looking up at young women walking on the surface of the earth, and I understood more about Persephone than I ever had before.

"There's not much left," my mother finally said, and I nodded. And I thought that when you lose the people close to you, become a single soul in this world, there isn't much left—that a soul isn't much by itself, and it's even less when it loses the memory of the things that formed it.

"You're here, aren't you?" asked my mother. "You're all right?"

"I'm all right," I said. "Julie and I are fine."

She smiled. "Good," she said. Then she said, "you should enjoy life while you're young," and I nodded at her one more time, determined to follow her advice, at least to the extent I could as a fifty-nine-year-old vessel of good intentions gone awry, and as a chronicler and a bearer of grief.

Rules for Writers

Orpheus's Ten Tips for Getting There and Getting Back with a Story

1. If it were easy to get to the unconscious, your mother wouldn't be guarding the entrance. To get to depth, you'll have to write about her sooner or later, in fiction or nonfiction, as character or setting or plot.

2. Unlived lives are sometimes more real than the other kind. When you write fiction, write about your real life, even if you haven't lived it.

3. Try this thought experiment if you think you've lived the only life you could: imagine the life your mother would have lived if she hadn't become a mother.

4. Every story has a doorway down. It's easy to miss it if you don't see it. It's easy to avoid it if you do see it. If you're having trouble ending a story, back up to the place where you think that doorway down might be. Look for it and walk through it.

5. Writers, when things are going well, get their images from the unconscious. If your mother appears in a dream and hands you something or tells you something, she's given you a story. Take it and turn your gaze toward your readers. You've gotten what you came for, whether you know it or not.

6. The unconscious is a place where space and time don't exist. Every conscious technical skill that you've learned or will

learn as a writer—plotting, advancing the story through dialogue, writing and rewriting a story's ending until you get it right, even writing simple, clear sentences and coherent paragraphs—all these are what you do to let a story exist in time and space. A narrative line is a series of conscious decisions.

7. Metaphors are fundamentally untrustworthy. They're lies. Never use them for their own sake, or because they're pretty. If you're going to use a metaphor, think like Iago, and use your lie to a greater purpose.

8. Learn to turn your face toward the things that nobody else wants to look at. You'll find things there that nobody else has seen.

9. Owning your story is a less happy circumstance than having a story own you. The slave always knows more about the master than the master knows about the slave.

10. A good story will always preserve the complexity and mystery of the thing that it's about.

10

Writing Grief

As many farewells as be stars in heaven.
—Shakespeare, *Troilus and Cressida*

I HAD TOLD THE STUDENTS in my undergraduate fiction workshop to write what they knew, and I was paying for it.

One fraternity boy submitted a long story about a fraternity boy who loses his girlfriend and spends the rest of the semester watching professional wrestling.

A girl brought a story about two girls shopping for shoes at a mall and getting in trouble with their parents for spending too much money.

A girl on the softball team came with a story about Billy the Baseball and Gary the Glove and Bobby the Bat and Ollie the Outfield. Billy and Gary and Bobby and Ollie were all good friends, friends for nine long innings.

At this point, the one nontraditional student in the class stood up and said she had something to say. She was a woman in her forties who had worked as a waitress to put her husband through med school. Then her husband had run off with one of his nurses. I had a good idea what the story she would submit to workshop would be about.

But she wasn't talking about doctors and nurses.

"The trouble with you kids," she yelled, "is that you didn't have a Vietnam War."

There was a shocked silence, and then she said, "You've never had to take anything seriously. You've never lost anything. You've never had to face anything you didn't want to. No wonder you can't write."

Up to that point, I had planned on telling the fraternity boy that his story should be about a failed professional wrestler dumped by his girlfriend. He would get a haircut, buy a couple of tailored suits, have his tattoos removed by laser, take elocution lessons, and work for an escort service, which is how he would become the love-slave of Antonin Scalia.

And the mall story might involve a shoe salesman with a serious patent-leather fetish, and the girls of the story might be undercover mall detectives who accept his invitation to go back with him to his apartment, where they discover thousands of stolen shoes and the mummified body of Imelda Marcos.

I was going to suggest that Bobby the Bat might have been corked and that Billy the Baseball was really Sammy the Spitball, and that they'd been shooting steroids more or less constantly since Boston had traded them to the Yankees.

But my older student changed all that. The classroom floor had opened up and we had all fallen into a deeper and darker place. It's mostly fortunate when that happens in a writing class.

"What do you think?" I asked the class. "Does loss make you a better writer?"

"I lost my Grandma," said a student.

"My hamster died," said another.

"I broke up with my girlfriend," said the fraternity boy.

These people were over eighteen, but calling them boys and girls wasn't off the mark. If there was real grief in their lives, I decided, their relationship to it was suspect. Between them and grief lay self-pity.

"Why wish a war on these nice young people?" I asked the woman, who was still standing.

"I lost a brother in Vietnam," she said. "I've written a story about him. It's about how good he was and how it must have torn him apart to kill people and how much the world lost and my parents lost when he died. I'm sorry, but I don't think you kids can understand that story." She sat down.

If you can stand it, a good thing to do in a writing class is to let silence go on and on.

"Can you understand her story?" I finally asked.

"My father died in Vietnam," said a girl.

"My father came back, but Mom says he's never been the same," said the fraternity boy. "He's crawled into a bottle."

"My brother died in a car accident," said a girl. "My other brother was driving."

"My grandmother has Alzheimer's. My grandfather died trying to care for her. Now she's in a nursing home and cries for him all the time."

There were other stories. They were better and sadder stories than people had previously brought before the workshop, and I wanted them all to go home and write those stories down. I decided that the unbearable mediocrity of most undergraduate workshop stories—and maybe the unbearable mediocrity of most American lives—was a defense against an ever-present grief.

"Bring your story in," I told the woman. "We'll come up with a war somehow."

EVERY WRITER should spend time thinking about grief and writing, and about how a writer always writes from within the matrix of his or her own life. All too often we can write a story in the direction of more and more meaning and depth until it reaches our own grief—or our family's or our culture's grief—and then we stop writing or the story becomes about something else and floats back up to the surface of things. Writers should also consider how to keep readers reading when a story brings them close to their own griefs, because so much of what we call everyday life in this country looks like distraction from grief. We have plastic crap in our shopping carts and pictures of Internet porn and unreal reality shows on the 51-inch flat-panel TVs in our living rooms so we can avoid thinking about the things that make us weep.

To better understand the relationship between grief and writing, I want to discuss *Gilgamesh*, which is the oldest story in the world. I'd also like you to look at the beauty and power of Stephen Mitchell's translation, for the pure pleasure of it and for the sure knowledge that good writing can reach across hundreds of generations to move your heart.

Gilgamesh is about the king of the ancient city of Uruk, Gilgamesh, the strongest of men—"huge, handsome, radiant, perfect"—and the death of his friend, brother, and lover, the wild man Enkidu, and Gilgamesh's inconsolable grief.

In a passage that encapsulates this understanding of the

book, Gilgamesh, crazed by Enkidu's death, is refused entrance
to a tavern because he looks so frightening that he must be a
murderer. Gilgamesh demands entrance as a king. The woman
who owns the tavern first asks him if he's a king, why he looks so
bad. Gilgamesh replies:

> Shouldn't my cheeks be hollow, shouldn't my face be
> ravaged, frost-chilled and burnt by the desert sun? Shouldn't
> my heart be filled with grief? Shouldn't I be worn out and
> ready to collapse? My friend, my brother Enkidu, whom
> I loved so dearly, who accompanied me through every
> danger—the fate of mankind has overwhelmed him.
>
> For six days I would not let him be buried, thinking, "If
> my grief is violent enough, perhaps he will come back to life
> again." For six days and seven nights I mourned him, until a
> maggot fell out of his nose.
>
> Then I was frightened, terrified by death, and I set out
> to roam the wilderness. I cannot bear what happened to my
> friend—I cannot bear what happened to Enkidu—so I roam
> the wilderness in my grief. How can my mind have any rest?
> My beloved friend has turned into clay—my beloved Enkidu
> has turned into clay. And won't I too lie down in the dirt like
> him, and never arise again?

This passage is the balance point of *Gilgamesh*. If we say that
Moby Dick is about a whale, we can say that *Gilgamesh* is about
a maggot. If Ahab saw his rage mirrored in the blank whiteness of the whale's forehead, Gilgamesh sees his grief mirrored
in that moment when the maggot falls out of Enkidu's nose.
In *Moby Dick,* everything that comes before the vision of the

whale's forehead is prologue, everything after is the working out of inevitabilities. In *Gilgamesh*, everything before the maggot is hope, everything after is defeat.

If you look at both these works as a writer interested in structure, you see that each story slowly brings the reader to a single reality-changing image, one until then hidden just below the surface, and then spends the rest of the time exploring how that now conscious image changes things for everyone forever. When the maggot falls out of Enkidu's nose, his death becomes undeniable, and an ever-present grief—even though it is inter-woven with self-pity—comes to consciousness.

THE PLOT OF *GILGAMESH* does not run the way heroic plots are supposed to run. In its structure, it runs counter to the story of the hero summarized by Joseph Campbell in *Hero With A Thousand Faces*. Instead of an ordinary man becoming a hero, a hero becomes an ordinary man. Gilgamesh's grief is sparked by the knowledge that he, too, will die. After he finally admits Enkidu is dead, Gilgamesh goes on a great quest for the plant that confers immortality. He finds it, but puts it down for a while and wanders off and a snake eats it. Immortality is lost to humanity forever. Gilgamesh becomes a fool—a tricked trickster—rather than a hero. The story *Gilgamesh* becomes not just about Enkidu's death but about Gilgamesh's eventual death, and about all of our deaths.

But *Gilgamesh* is not a nice simple God-Bites-Man tale like *Moby Dick*. There are other images that transform its reality, and other understandings of its story. It's a book about civilization, and about how civilizations cut themselves off from their life-blood. To look at how this happens we need to look at another image that rises to the surface earlier in the story.

Enkidu really is a wild man, created by the gods to serve as a man equal to Gilgamesh, who as the story begins is abusing the people he rules. In the words of the story, "he takes the son from his father and crushes him, takes the girl from her mother and uses her, the warrior's daughter, the young man's bride, he uses her, no one dares to oppose him. Is this how you want your king to rule? Should a shepherd savage his own flock?"

Gilgamesh is sexually insatiable. He demands to mate with the city's brides on the first night of marriage. He wears the young men out in athletic contests. When Enkidu is created as a kind of untamed mirror image of Gilgamesh, it is as though what is outside the city walls of Uruk gains a power equal to what is within. When word of a wild man reaches the city, he is seen as a threat to both Gilgamesh and to civilization. Remember that this is a time when civilization has not proven that it has any staying power, and if you have a strong king, it is worthwhile to put up with his quirks or at least ask the gods to deal with him in a way that gets rid of the quirks but maybe keeps the king.

Gilgamesh is as canny as he is strong and good-looking. Rather than confronting this wild man himself, he sends the wise and experienced temple prostitute Shamhat, a priestess of the love and fertility goddess Ishtar, to go into the wilderness and tame Enkidu and make him fit for civilization. Here is what happens when she reaches the waterhole where Enkidu drinks with his animal friends:

> She stripped off her robe and lay there naked, with
> her legs apart, touching herself. Enkidu saw her and warily

approached. He sniffed the air. He gazed at her body. He
drew close. Shamhat touched him on the thigh, touched his
penis, and put him inside her.

She used her love-arts, she took his breath with her
kisses, held nothing back, and showed him what a woman is.
For seven days he stayed erect and made love with her, until
he had had enough. At last he stood up and walked toward
the waterhole to rejoin his animals. But the gazelles saw
him and scattered, the antelope and deer bounded away. He
tried to catch up, but his body was exhausted, his life force
was spent, he could no longer run like an animal, as he had
before. He turned back to Shamhat, and as he walked he
knew that his mind had somehow grown larger. He knew
things now that an animal can't know.

In any other story, this passage would be the great transforming image of the book. But once Shamhat's job is done, the story
ignores her. She is dismissed, and it's Enkidu who dismisses her.
He does it first by cursing her, and then, in a quick reversal, by
blessing her. He himself is dying of a curse at the time, so he has
the right to be a little confused and angry.

Enkidu and Gilgamesh have gone to a sacred forest and
killed its divine protector, the demon Humbaba. But Humbaba
has lived long enough to curse Enkidu to death.

Enkidu also takes a little while to die. He thinks back to the
earlier event that has led him to his end. He says:

Shamhat, I assign you an eternal fate, I curse you with
the ultimate curse, may it seize you instantly, as it leaves
my mouth. Never may you have a home and family, never

caress a child of your own, may your man prefer younger, prettier girls, may he beat you as a housewife beats a rug, may you never acquire bright alabaster or shining silver, may your roof keep leaking and no carpenter fix it, may wild dogs camp in your bedroom, may owls nest in your attic, may drunkards vomit all over you, may a tavern wall be your place of business, may you be dressed in torn robes and filthy underwear, may angry wives sue you, may thorns and briars make your feet bloody, may young men jeer and the rabble mock you as you walk the streets. Shamhat, may all this be your reward for seducing me in the wilderness when I was young and strong and innocent and free.

But a curse like this involves the gods, and a god's voice reminds Enkidu of the benefits that came with his domestication: bread, and beer, and fine clothing, and the intimate friendship of Gilgamesh, and finally a fine funeral with Gilgamesh as the chief mourner. Enkidu thinks a minute and says:

Shamhat, I assign you a different fate, my mouth that cursed you will bless you now. May you be adored by nobles and princes, two miles away from you may your lover tremble with excitement, one mile away may he bite his lip in anticipation, may the warrior long to be naked beside you, may Ishtar give you generous lovers whose treasure chests brim with jewels and gold, may the mother of seven be abandoned for your sake.

After receiving that curiously contemporary curse and blessing, Shamhat disappears from the story.

THESE PASSAGES find an echo, five thousand years later, in our cultural attitudes toward female sexuality. About the same time I was in cold and snowy central Idaho, sitting next to a wood-stove and reading Enkidu's blessing and his curse, Paris Hilton and Britney Spears were nightclubbing in L.A., giving up underwear altogether, and letting paparazzi take photos of their nether regions. Along with a few billion other people, I viewed those photos on the Internet. You can too, if you want, although it may take you a while to find them. Googling Britney Spears will call up 52.2 million entries, and Paris Hilton will call up 36 million.

What I was struck by, other than the clear evidence that both Britney Spears and Paris Hilton are female, was their unconscious reenactment of a five-thousand-year-old conscious ritual. Shamhat was a prostitute commanded by her king to make a wild man fit for civilization. For her efforts, she received a bad curse and a dubious blessing, but that did not matter as much as the fact that everything she did was connected to the divine. All that she did was sacred. She allowed men a connection to Ishtar, and through Ishtar, to the fertility of their flocks and fields, to their own sexuality, and to an everlasting cycle of decay and renewal.

But what was sacred and conscious in Uruk is profane and unconscious in L.A., and probably missing any final blessing or transition from decay to renewal. If a young woman evokes Ishtar in twenty-first century America, we find ourselves waiting for the overdose, the fatal car accident, the eating disorder, the sudden conversion to Christianity, the revelation of children duct-taped to their beds on club night. That bright flame that so fascinates us in those young women will be made into something we can scorn or forget.

We've seen it before, when Jayne Mansfield was decapitated when her car ran into a truck. Marilyn Monroe, who played temple priestess to a playwright and baseball hero and president and attorney general, either killed herself or was murdered. Janis Joplin overdosed. Princess Diana died chased by paparazzi. And Anna Nicole Smith. All these women held a female energy that our culture is truly comfortable with only as long as it's dead. No one can be allowed to possess it for long. If it's not destroyed outright, it's made grotesque.

It may seem a long leap from Shamhat to Paris Hilton getting out of a limousine. It might seem just as long a leap from Paris Hilton or even Princess Diana to the image of Lynndie England torturing prisoners at Abu Ghraib.

But the photo of Lynndie England pointing at the genitals of a naked and hooded Iraqi prisoner, a cigarette sticking out of her smile, became the icon of the Iraq War. This is what divine female sexuality looks like in the service of a culture that cannot allow any conscious connection between the divine and the female and sexuality. We've come a long way from Shamhat and Ishtar. We've come a long way toward death and grief, but we're not about to admit that.

THERE'S ANOTHER PASSAGE from *Gilgamesh* worth examining. It comes after Gilgamesh and Enkidu have fought and become friends and lovers. It comes after they have become bored with the luxuries of Uruk and have sought adventure. They have traveled to the sacred forest, killed Humbaba, and cut down the cedars and brought them back to Uruk for the city's gates.

Gilgamesh comes home, washes off Humbaba's blood, puts on

new clothes and his crown. He's headed out for a night on the town with Enkidu, but the goddess Ishtar, whose temple is the finest building in Uruk, finally notices him. She likes what she sees:

> "Come here, Gilgamesh," Ishtar said, "marry me, give me your luscious fruits, be my husband, be my sweet man...and I will bless everything you own. Your goats will bear triplets, your ewes will twin, your donkeys will be faster than any mule, your chariot-horses will win every race, your oxen will be the envy of the world. These are the least of the gifts I will shower upon you. Come here. Be my sweet man."

Here is yet another image that should work as a pivot for the story, and if it had, the epic of Gilgamesh would be about a hero that through his virtue and strength, married a goddess and brought her blessings to his people.

But Gilgamesh refuses her. He's not going to be anybody's sweet man except Enkidu's. He says:

> "Why would I want to be the lover of a broken oven that fails in the cold, a flimsy door that the wind blows through, a palace that falls on its staunchest defenders, a mouse that gnaws through its thin reed shelter, tar that blackens the workman's hands, a waterskin that is full of holes and leaks all over its bearer, a piece of limestone that crumbles and undermines a solid stone wall, a battering ram that knocks down the rampart of an allied city, a shoe that mangles its owner's foot?"

Gilgamesh then reminds her about what has happened to all her previous husbands, who were pathetically domesticated or killed when Ishtar grew bored with them. Ishtar gets enraged, goes back to heaven and begs her father, the great god Anu, for the Bull of Heaven. She says if she doesn't get it, she will smash the gates to the underworld and let the dead out to devour the living. It's the first account of a George Romero movie in literature.

Anu lets Ishtar have the Bull, but when it goes down to earth to punish Gilgamesh, Enkidu and Gilgamesh kill it. When Ishtar, who is dismayed by this development, stands wailing on the wall of Uruk, Enkidu rips off a hind quarter of the Bull and flings it in her face. Together, Gilgamesh and Enkidu wash off the Bull's blood in the river and return to the city, hand in hand. They ride a chariot through cheering crowds.

But then Enkidu has a dream that killing Humbaba and cutting down the Sacred Cedar Forest and slaughtering the Bull of Heaven has—for some reason—offended the gods. And the gods *are* offended. They decree that Humbaba's curse on Enkidu will be carried out.

Ishtar does not disappear from the narrative as completely as her priestess. After Enkidu dies, Gilgamesh offers her a polished cedar javelin so she will walk at Enkidu's side in the underworld. And the story ends with the same words that started it: a song of praise to the great city of Uruk, with the same mention of the Temple of Ishtar, which no king can equal in size or beauty. But as a character in the story, as someone who can affect its outcome for better or for worse, Ishtar disappears as completely as Shamhat. Uruk has lost its goddess.

SCHOLARS WHO STUDY *Gilgamesh* talk about the complexity of its plot. But when you write and rewrite stories, you get a sense of what a story wants to be and you do your best to bring it into being in just that way. Usually some of what a story wants to be involves a symmetry between levels of meaning, and *Gilgamesh* isn't symmetrical in that way. If it were, we might expect to see Gilgamesh and Shamhat together in the end, and be witness to her love arts taming not the wildness of the wild man on the first level of the story but the wildness of Gilgamesh's grief on a subsequent level.

But instead we have a story whose symmetries have never been completed, or once complete, have been destroyed. What has been destroyed by the end of *Gilgamesh* is any connection between the sacred and the feminine. Ishtar has been insulted, and her flocks and crops and sexuality have been given over to her father, Anu.

Shamhat has been reduced from the level of priestess to the level of whore. The surface of the story suddenly concerns only what exists between men, not between men and women. There is grief in this scheme of things, grief that comes from a lack of the feminine. That is a bigger absence than anyone in the story realizes. Gilgamesh has refused Ishtar because he sees her as a goddess of death. He has forgotten that she's a goddess of life as well.

When Gilgamesh finally looks on his great city again—after he has lost Enkidu and has traveled to the ends of the earth for the plant that will confer immortality and through his carelessness has lost it—he looks upon it with the knowledge that he must someday leave its walls, its beautiful young men and women, its temples, its celebrations and its laughter, this time when he dies, this time for all time. And there is the greater knowledge of the story itself that Uruk, the city, lacking the favor of Ishtar and her ability to endlessly renew life, will itself return to dust.

So the complexity of the plot of *Gilgamesh* is found in what is missing from it rather than in its elaborate and imaginative sub-plots. But when you cut a passage from a story, it still exists in the story. You might say it exists in the story's unconscious, where it can often exert more power than if it were there on the page.

One axiom of craft that you can take from this reading of *Gilgamesh* is that a story will never achieve the power you want for it unless you've cut a lot out of it. It's an exercise that causes a lot of grief for a writer, at least until you realize your murdered darlings are still there in the story's unconscious.

THERE ARE OTHER GRIEFS that you as a writer need to face. You owe it to your readers to face them. At the start of this chapter I mentioned mediocrity—a studied ordinariness—as a defense against an ever-present grief. But when you first encounter Gilgamesh in his agony of loss, there is a shock of recognition. The more you've pushed any knowledge of death—any 3 A.M. vision of the maggot—from your life, the greater that shock can be.

The students in my undergraduate workshop came from a culture where the knowledge of death was almost completely suppressed, and it took an angry grieving woman and a long period of silence to get them to recover any consciousness of what they had loved and lost.

So here's another axiom of craft: when we deal with the shock of the new we invent things that no one has ever seen before. The effect on our audience is to make them realize how new things can be, and how imagination can extend the universe.

But when we deal with the shock of recognition, the effect on our audience is to make them remember things that they've forgotten, and usually there are good reasons they've forgotten them. It's much more dangerous to be a shock-of-recognition artist than a daring avant-garde shock-of-the-new artist, and not just because you anger people by reminding them of things that they've pushed out of their minds.

The blind spots we all have are openings to the underworld. As a writer, you can walk into them. But the reason the I—the ego—gets scared at the first step down is that the ego cannot exist in the underworld. From a writing standpoint, the ego needs to take the form of a narrative voice to order and make sense of unconscious material. You can't write out of the underworld and you can't write out of blind spots. You have to descend, but you also have to come back out, and then you have to work on what you brought back so it becomes accessible to people who can't enter their blind spots and so cannot ever go to the underworld. That's what the artist who works with the shock of recognition does.

HERE IS ANOTHER axiom of craft: it is better to write as a whole person than half a person. To understand this idea, we need to explore what the suppression of the divine feminine does to the writer. It limits the scope of our art and the potential of our characters.

Contemporary American models for the divine feminine are limited. There's the Virgin Mary, who exists almost as an abstract, although if we become more conscious of her grief we find she exists in a few places as The Black Madonna. There are female astronauts. There's *Venus* Williams. There are hints of Sophia and Lilith in the Old Testament.

Then there's Mother Teresa, and one article I saw on Paris Hilton stated she has a startling resemblance to Mother Teresa as a young woman, which was a stunningly effective way to obliterate Paris Hilton's youth and sexuality. But it also points out a way that Paris Hilton might save herself from becoming the sacrifice she's about to become: she can marry an absent male God. I suspect Paris Hilton would rather be a sacrifice than make such a sacrifice.

Among contemporary writers who evoke the divine feminine, Margaret Atwood comes to mind, but, less happily, so do the science fiction writer James Tiptree, Jr., Zelda Fitzgerald, Anne Sexton, Sylvia Plath and Emily Dickinson. Among visual artists, Georgia O'Keefe stands almost alone as a true avatar of Ishtar, and the power of her floral paintings can make you cry out in pain because in their shadows you see things you should never have been so careless as to have lost.

THE BIGGEST SOURCE of unending but unconscious grief in my undergraduate workshop was not the death or absence of loved ones, but the absence of any connection to Ishtar and the possibility of renewal that she once offered. Because Ishtar has been banished from our daylit world, we don't even know enough to name what we're grieving.

But we do grieve for her. Her absence causes the same horrible relations between men and women in our world as it did in Gilgamesh's world. We act out that grief in our jobs, in our relationships, and we flinch when we brush up against our own unlived lives—if those lives exist in an alternate universe where Ishtar is still present.

IT'S A HARD THING to perceive any of this when your culture is a patriarchy dedicated to an abstract and absent god. As Jung said, it's hard to see the lion that has swallowed you.

Becoming a whole person is not easy to do in a patriarchy. Whether you define yourself as with it or against it, the culture is a mirror you see yourself in, and in our case it's only a fragment of mirror, and we see only a fragment of ourselves.

Louise J. Kaplan, in her controversial book *Female Perversions,* uses the character Madame Bovary to bolster her thesis that women in western culture have become female impersonators, and the female persona each one adopts fits one of a limited number of patriarchal definitions. Deborah Tannen, in an essay titled "Marked Women, Unmarked Men" makes a number of these definitions explicit, and we recognize them immediately.

Men, of course, have their own problems with being defined as half-people by the patriarchy, and a good many of them are right now in Iraq and Afghanistan, choking on the dust of Uruk and other cities that once worshipped the Divine Feminine. We have come up with a war for them, and I suspect that as a culture we've become more comfortable with grieving over their broken bodies than we are with grieving the loss of Ishtar.

WHEN I TALK with writers about the loss of Ishtar, I talk about the need to get in touch with their inner nasty high-school girl.

That's neither a kind nor an enlightened way to put it, but it gets the idea across. There are only a few places where Ishtar can truly be these days, and high school is one of them. She appears briefly, in young women whose sexuality comes on them like a whirlwind and who, in the absence of ritual, serve as unconscious vessels for Ishtar until she tires of them and breaks them and throws them aside. It is not a good thing for the people it possesses, this goddess energy, especially in collusion with a culture that needs a constant supply of grim object lessons to enforce its standards of behavior upon its citizens.

And yet this energy of the goddess can save a life—your life, especially if you're a writer, because it's an energy of renewal, and while one of our essential jobs is to grieve for the world, another is to renew the world, to pick up the broken things and put them back together again. That putting things back together is what writers do in the face of death and grief, and it's nice to have Ishtar at your side when you're picking through the shards, looking for edges that fit together.

In the absence of ancient priestesses, we all have to find our own paths to Ishtar. In the absence of ancient ritual, we have to construct our own.

If you're a writer, that means that you owe your stories whole women characters, and you owe those characters a sacred moment—a moment of grief and renewal. You can't have the latter without the former.

No matter if these women are dead soldiers or the sisters or mothers or wives of dead soldiers, no matter if they're despised ex-lovers, no matter if they're the brutal guards in a prison, no matter if they're bitter divorcees on girls' night out, or exhausted housemaids, or single mothers with five children by five fathers, or CEOs of electronics companies or dying astronauts or muttering lumps in a nursing home or stick figures in an anorexia clinic—no matter who they are, you owe them this: the knowledge of that lost moment when they first knew their own sexuality, when they were too quick and free to embrace the world, when they moved with the awkward beautiful grace of youth, and when they saw the world through Ishtar's eyes: all green hills and ripe fields and clear flowing water, all full of the endless possibility of life.

If you can bring that image of the divine feminine into the consciousness of your wild reader, his mind will somehow have grown larger. He will know things then that an animal can't know. And you will have shown him what a writer is.

Rules for Writers

Ishtar's Ten Commandments for Writing in a World Too Long Deprived of Renewal

1. Face the grief in your characters and the sadness in their stories if you want to write stories that come to a satisfactory end.

2. Recognize that grief is part of the writing experience. You'll experience it in the writing of every story.

3. Don't scorn the old gods and goddesses, even when they show up drunk or angry.

4. Over time, a writing career will acquaint you with your own grief and anger. Admit it. Embrace it. Write it.

5. Grieve for the world as it was before civilization cut its forests, domesticated its animals, paved its meadows, and oiled its beaches.

6. Don't write like a man. The feminine represents connection to the divine, to fertility, to sexuality, and to an everlasting cycle of decay and renewal.

7. If there's an easy way and a hard way to write something, take the hard way. The unbearable mediocrity of many stories (and many lives) is a willingness to be distracted from what Jung called legitimate suffering.

8. Make your readers remember things that they've forgotten. It will be good for them, and with luck, they'll forgive you before you die.

9. Treat your readers with respect. They don't have the time to know what you know. Your own arrogance can kill the best parts of your stories.

10. Don't fear the death of a story. That moment where a story roars back to life, having been given up for dead, is the moment when you realize that it's the story's will to live, not your will to write it, that's important.

Epilogue
Writing Travel

Kids, don't try this at home.

YOU RENEW YOUR PASSPORT, you buy a plane ticket, you grab a notebook and a pen. You get off the plane and you start taking notes on what you see and hear and smell and taste and touch. You make sure all your sentences make sense and your paragraphs cohere. Do this long enough and surface will yield to depth. What could possibly go wrong?

Item: The Travel Writer writes a lead in the first person confidential.

I'm in Prachuap Kiri Khan, a small fishing village a day's train ride south of Bangkok. A morning breeze is blowing in from the Gulf of Siam, picking up spray from the waves crashing into the seawall. It's cooling the open balcony where I'm sitting in shorts and T-shirt at a polished teak table, holding a pen and staring at the empty lines of a legal tablet. I've left my laptop at home because I've found that a computer can distort my perceptions of almost everything. My perceptions need to be protected, because they're all that I have to sell to the editors at *Travel & Leisure,* if and when they reply to my query email.

The balcony is just outside my room at the Sun Beach Resort, a ten-room boutique hotel done in Portuguese Colonial style— yellow stucco walls punctuated by white fluted columns and sculpted window frames. The balconies and the rooms they're attached to are floored with pale blue tile. The tile is warm where the sun hits it, but the heat feels good to my bare feet. This morning I bought a half-hour of Internet on the Sun Beach's computer, perceptions be damned, and I checked the weather at home. Thirty-two below, Fahrenheit.

Below my balcony is the Sun Beach swimming pool, and a beautiful and once very white, now slightly pink woman in a black bikini and sunglasses lies on a chaise longue, reading—I can read the title from here—John LeCarre's *Tailor of Panama.* Beyond the pool is a masonry wall. Beyond the wall is the shore road. Beyond the shore road is Prachuap Kiri Khan's mile-long promenade, and beyond that is the Gulf. There is no beach. The waves hit high up the seawall, and they're big enough that they would be dangerous to swim in. At night, when the tide goes out, there is a beach, but there's no sun.

Item: Timing is everything.

It's the last day of November, but by mid-December or January, when the tourists are supposed to start hitting Thailand in earnest, there will be simultaneous beach and sun, and the other nine rooms of the Sun Beach, now mostly empty, will be filled with Germans and a Frenchman. I make this assumption based on the books in the hotel library, a small bookcase in the lobby, which has several hundred books in German, and a French automobile magazine. However, the family below us in the hotel is Dutch.

The Thai woman who owns the place is friendly and speaks English. She has three children: a girl of eight or nine, a boy about twelve, and a girl of fifteen or sixteen. The older girl helps with the accounts and motorbike rentals. The younger one helps one of the maids with the laundry. The boy disappears during school hours. There's also a young unshaven German guy in a T-shirt and ragged shorts whom I've seen at a table in the lobby. The table has always held a pint of cheap Mekong rice whiskey, a bucket of ice, and a two-liter bottle of Pepsi. I decide the German has come to Thailand because his unemployment stipends go further here than in Frankfurt. The Dutch family doesn't speak to him, even though their languages sound the same to me.

It's good to be here in November. By mid-December, the staff will be less happy to see tourists. High-season fatigue will set in. People who work in the hospitality industry become statisticians, and chart trends and make judgments. Americans are one thing, Germans another, the French something else besides. As a tourist, you are forced into a mold that other tourists before you have already constructed, and usually that mold hasn't been created by good behavior.

Item: The Travel Writer submits a query.

If you go to the *Travel & Leisure* website, you can query the editors with story ideas. In theory, it should be a fast and efficient method of getting a story assigned to you. Send in your story idea, and a *Travel & Leisure* intern, a Sarah Lawrence creative writing major, looks at it, and gets excited about the idea of reporting on a small and scintillatingly clean hotel in a small fishing village on the Gulf of Siam, where motorbike trips can be taken to the local caves and temples, and fresh-caught seafood is sold in the promenade cafés. And there's sea-kayaking out to the islands in the bay, and snorkeling above pristine coral reefs.

The intern bursts into an editorial planning meeting, where the senior editors, the managing editor, and the publisher and assistant publishers are trying to plan an issue that won't be as boring as the last one.

"I've got someone who wants to do a story on Thailand," says the intern. "He's going there anyway, so we won't have to buy his plane ticket."

"Yes!" say the editors and publishers, all leaping to their feet. "Thailand! The food! The beaches! The temples! The coral reefs! The small perfect hotels with balconies above the promenades! Why didn't we think of that before?"

Item: *The Travel Writer tries to get to know his audience.*

That's what all this staring at the blank page is all about. I need to know whom I'm writing for. Is it the editors sitting in an office high above New York's Avenue of the Americas? Or is it the subscribers to *Travel & Leisure,* or the subset of *Travel & Leisure* subscribers who actually *buy* the stuff advertised on its slick pages, the Louis Vuitton bags, the Lexuses and the BMWs, the Cartier watches, the thousand-dollar-a-night hotel rooms?

A couple of questions for these high-end consumers: What unappeasable unconscious hunger possesses you to buy all that frippery and crap anyway? Haven't you read Thorstein Veblen's *The Theory of the* Travel & Leisure *Class*?

Not a question that the editors and publishers of *Travel & Leisure* will ask their readers. So forget I said it. Instead, assume that everyone, no matter how rich and unselfconscious, will care about money. Let's look at some prices: our hotel room is costing the two of us twenty-seven dollars a night. A full-course meal in a Prachuap Kiri Khan restaurant is five or six dollars. All day on a motorbike is nine dollars, although if you wreck it you buy it. The rental contract is quite specific on that point.

Item: The Travel Writer, trying to solve the audience problem, switches to the Second Person Coercive.

You are on the balcony of a small and exquisite hotel in Thailand, sitting in bright sunshine that would be too warm if it weren't for the sea breeze wafting in off the Gulf of Siam—

Wait a minute.

The travel writer objects to your use of the word, "wafting." It's not a word he would be caught dead using. And it's really his article, even though he's pretending that it's your perceptions that are important here. He thinks you should use a word less redolent of odor, even though the sea breeze does smell a bit like fish, but it's not unpleasant at all, and besides, the bay's background essence of creatures being born and dying and rotting and being born again out of the rot—that's not what we're reporting on here. It's the cooling effect of the breeze that's—

that's *ripping* in from the Gulf of Siam.

"But it's not ripping," you say. "If it were ripping I wouldn't be on the balcony. The legal tablet would be blowing all over and impossible to write on."

Then it dawns on you that you're not the travel writer anyway, you're just the poor construct that the travel writer has invented to write his article for him. Forget this, you decide. It's time to walk into town for a beer. You leave the balcony and walk downstairs past the woman in the black bikini. As you pass her, you drop your room key on the chaise longue beside her.

"I will return to my room this afternoon," you say to her. "I would be only too delighted to find you there when I open the door. I will bring beer. Premium beer."

She says nothing. Her book has fallen to her side. You realize she may be sleeping.

You shrug and continue past the pool and across the shore road to the promenade. There, in between racks of filleted fish drying in the sun, high waves have tossed flotsam onto the concrete. You find empty disposable cigarette lighters, Styrofoam bits, pieces of plastic rope, net floats, cigarette butts, plastic bags, empty and torn swimsuits, more plastic bags, plastic bottles, plastic shoes, plastic toys, plastic sand, and dead crabs. What look like shiny coins waiting to be picked up are tiny round fish, also dead.

You continue down the promenade, passing a hotel or two, until you're opposite a sign that advertises a Thai-German restaurant. You go in, order a Heineken, and, after reading through pages and pages of menu, you order the schnitzel.

Item: The Travel Writer realizes his true audience.

It's the intern from Sarah Lawrence. It's her and her alone. The travel writer may think it's the editors, or the readers, or the publisher, but the guardian of the gate is the intern. Without willing it, the travel writer imagines her in too great of detail: her idea of foreign travel was formed between her last year of high school and her first year of college, when she spent a month in the South of France, courtesy of her investment banker father's American Express card, drinking coffee and writing postcards at sidewalk cafes in the mornings, and visiting small museums, with their Picassos and Rousseaus and Matisses, in the afternoons. As a writer, she hopes to channel Grace Paley, or Albert Camus. For her, irony is a historical phenomenon.

The travel writer starts a new lead: "In those early days of the pandemic, the easiest way of making Prachuap Kiri Khan's acquaintance was to ascertain how the people in it worked, how they loved, and how they died."

Another new lead: "I saw my wife on a chaise longue beside the pool. I was sitting on the balcony of our hotel. Hello, my life, I said. We have been married thirteen years, so I felt justified. She said, I'm not your life. Even so, you could make the life you do have better if you went into town and got us some beer. So I did, hoping to find some schnitzel on the way."

That doesn't work either. And the travel writer shudders to think what the intern will think of the dead crabs and fish and plastic trash that have washed up on the promenade, or the stacks of fish reeking in the sun, or of eating schnitzel in a country famous for its Tom Yum Goong and Pad Thai. She's not going to like these details at all, and she's going to delete the travel writer's query before the editors have a chance to see it.

Item: Travel & Leisure *hasn't responded to the query.*

Maybe the intern was sick that day. Maybe the editors have all been laid off. Maybe the magazine is being targeted at a new demographic, one younger and less comfortable with paragraphs. It happens. When *Skiing Magazine* aimed itself at 18- to 24-year-olds, it stopped using big words and replaced articles with photo essays with the word "Dude!" in their titles. Maybe *Travel & Leisure* has decided to cater to that subset of its readers that buys its advertised products but prefers to stay home, frightened at the thought of getting on a plane or passing through customs or catching tropical parasites that would build condos in their livers.

It's true that there have been articles lately about places in Bhutan and Burma where almost no one can get to. There have been stories of kidnappings of tourists, and antibiotic resistance to lethal germs, botched plastic surgeries in foreign clinics, and fines and jail terms for violation of obscure marriage customs.

The travel writer wishes he had the number of a senior editor to call. He used to, but turnover of senior editors is high—being an intern is a more secure position—and everyone he used to work with is gone.

Item: *Desperate to get some facts on the page, the Travel Writer breaks down and switches to the Third Person Mundane.*

Prachuap Kiri Khan is a city of thirty thousand on the Gulf

of Siam. Its name in Thai means Land of Many Mountains, a reference to the many limestone hills and steep cliffs that form the local geography. Besides being the seat of provincial government, it is home to Wing 5 of the Thai Air Force, a reconnaissance and training squadron. It is situated at the east edge of the narrowest part of Thailand, about halfway to the Malaysian border from Bangkok. It is the point on the Malay Peninsula at which the Japanese invaded Thailand on December 8, 1941, and fought a brief battle with the air force garrison and the local militia before agreeing to a cease-fire the next day.

The city occupies the middle of three beautiful half-moon bays. The bays are dotted by small limestone islands, and divided from each other by headlands, and mostly bordered by broad white beaches and sea pines.

Local attractions include Wat Thammikaram, a complex of late nineteenth century temples atop the steep limestone hill that marks the center of town. One of the temples commemorates King Monkut, an amateur naturalist, who came to Prachuap Kiri Khan to view a total solar eclipse in 1868, caught malaria in the marshes south of the city, and died.

The northern headland contains a limestone cave that is reached by following a long set of concrete stairs three hundred feet up the hillside. The entrance is small and cramped, but the cave immediately opens up into large rooms twenty and thirty feet high, lit by dim fluorescent tubes. These rooms, a hundred yards or more of them, are filled with Buddha images, some of them reclining dusty and golden over fifty feet of rock, some of them sitting in rows like the terracotta figures in a Chinese emperor's tomb. Some of them are small and made of clear green glass, or corroding bronze, or dark stone, and hundreds of them peek out at visitors from between stalagmites.

Perhaps because of the military influence, the city has remained off the usual tourist routes, and there's less of a Western influence than in many Thai beach towns. Most of the tourists are from Bangkok, although some small hotels cater to westerners. In the city proper, there are three large Chinese-owned hotels and many smaller guest houses. Restaurants range from the formal dining rooms in the hotels to small hole-in-the-wall noodle shops. There's a Thai-German restaurant that serves schnitzel.

Item: The patron saint of Travel Writers is Marcus Aurelius.

Marcus Aurelius said in his *Meditations* that If It's Not Right, Don't Do It, and If It's Not the Truth, Don't Say It. Good advice for travel writers everywhere. I have a psychotherapist friend who says it's good advice for life itself, but we're dealing with stuff we can handle here.

But it really is important not to be a jerk when you're writing about a foreign country. You're setting up the dynamics for everyone who comes after you. The concepts that apply come from chaos theory: there's a sensitive dependence on initial conditions and an irresponsible universe keeps allowing travel writers to set the initial conditions.

I'm not kidding. Thomas Pynchon, in *V.* and *Gravity's Rainbow*, has invented a place called Baedekerland. Baedekerland is an alternate universe that has sprung into being because of the Baedeker guidebooks written for young people doing a grand tour of Europe in the nineteenth century. The Thailand equivalent is the

Lonely Planet guide to Thailand, and it describes a place that almost every visitor arriving at Bangkok's airport is headed to. You go where it tells you to go. You see what it tells you to see. You eat what it tells you to eat, and pronounce the Thai words for hello and thank you the way it tells you to pronounce them. *Lonely Planet Thailand* isn't Thailand, until you read it. Then it's the Thailand you can't escape.

Chaos theory also gives us the Butterfly Effect. If the flap of a butterfly's wings in Brazil can result in a tornado in Kansas ten days later, your being rude to a waiter today because he didn't understand your order might be transmuted, step by step, into nuclear war between India and Pakistan next month. In this view of things, there are no bit parts in travel writing, or in history either.

So tell the truth. Don't do things that are morally wrong. When and if your query gets through to the *Travel & Leisure* editors, they will remember, far back in their memories, when they, too, wanted to do the right thing and tell the truth, before their archived stories became their history, and before selling advertising became the paramount goal of the company. If you do the right thing and tell the truth, they will recognize in you some younger, less jaded, less ironic version of themselves. In a more just world, this recognition would cause them to rejoice in your work. As it happens, it just makes them angry at you.

Item: The Travel Writer reflects on his younger, less jaded, less ironic self.

Shortly after I acquired my MFA, my former professor Bill Kittredge called me up. Kittredge's reputation as a chronicler of the American West had reached the offices of *Travel & Leisure,* and its editors had commissioned him to write a brief overview of Montana, Wyoming, and Idaho. That overview would introduce three articles, each of them detailing the ten best places to visit in their respective states.

Kittredge wanted to know if I would do the Idaho piece. Thinking of *Outside Magazine,* I told him that I thought the ten-best article was a horrible, stupid form that had done more to damage the beautiful and rare places of the world than any number of clear cuts or dioxin dumps.

"They pay a dollar-fifty a word," he said.

"Where do I sign?" I asked.

After talking to the editor assigned to my piece, I got a map of Idaho and selected the ten most pristine hidden places my local's knowledge could identify. I wrote an outline, briefly sketching each location. Because I wanted to write the best 75,000-word expose of Idaho's beauty that had ever been written, I faxed the outline to my editor for her approval.

I got a phone call from her an hour after I'd sent the fax.

"It's fine. We'll take it," she said.

"I'll get right to work," I said.

There was silence on the phone. Finally she said, "I said we'd take it. You don't have to do anything else."

"You don't understand," I said. "That's my outline."

"*You* don't understand. That's your article."

So I made twelve hundred dollars for a half-hour's research and writing, and I hadn't worried over word choice or the amount of writer's intelligence it showed. I just looked it up and wrote it down. There's a lesson there: the editors of slick magazines want

your words to be long on information and short on beauty, reso-
nance, and irony. "Just the facts, Ma'am," says Sergeant Friday,
and he's happy that his job is to bully facts out of hysterical witnesses. He thinks back before he started police work to when he
was a senior editor at *Travel & Leisure*, trying to bully facts out
of travel writers, and shudders.

Item: The Travel Writer finds a story, but it's the wrong story.

We rent a motorbike for a day. Thais drive on the left side of the
road, so I drive and Julie navigates. In practice, this means that I
take us around a corner and Julie says, "Left. *Left. Left, damn it,*"
and I get back in our lane before the oncoming truck or tuk-tuk
or bus takes us out.

But we make it down to the air force base, which is open to
the public. At the guardhouse, the guard smiles and waves, and
we ride across the runway, which has caution signs indicating
that you shouldn't cross it when F-16s are taking off or landing.
We make our way past barracks and an open-air museum full of
ancient Curtis-Wright single-prop warplanes to a small park. In
the center of the park is a frieze carved into a sandstone monolith, and the frieze shows, on one side, the one-day battle the Prachuap Kiri Khan airmen and militia had with the invading Japanese. The Thais are armed with pistols and bolt-action rifles, the
Japanese with machine guns and a battleship. The other side of
the monolith records the signing of a cease-fire the next day. The
Thai generals look proud, the Thai soldiers stand fiercely next to
their Japanese counterparts, and the Thai civilians celebrate.

The sandstone does not explain that the Thais came into

the war on the side of the Japanese, and that the bridge over the river Kwai and the railroad that made it necessary were built with the slave labor of British and Dutch prisoners of war. By becoming allies of the Japanese, the Thais had saved their citizens from becoming slaves. Tens of thousands of POWs died of disease and torture and summary execution. At war's end, the British wanted to try Thai collaborators, including the king, as war criminals, but bowed to the Americans, who were already fighting the Cold War and wanted Thailand on their side.

There is a story here, a long and sad one full of blood and politics and purposely forgotten crimes, but it's not a story for *Travel & Leisure*. There's a reason I think that *Travel & Leisure* selects its interns from creative writing majors at Sarah Lawrence. They are the first line of defense against history.

Item: Failure is always an option in travel writing.

Five nights in Prachuap Kiri Khan, and the next morning we get on the train again. Julie is starting to get a tan, but that's not a story unless you know Julie. The cave full of Buddhas was nice, but after ten minutes of those smiling faces looking at you in the dim light, they start to look like evil clowns. The hotel has remained clean and friendly. We've found several great seafood restaurants, and we've learned that you can eat the whole of a scaly, primitive-looking fish, head, eyeballs, tail, and all, if it's covered with the right fluorescent orange sauce. The temple on the hill in the center of town is a good place to sit and watch the vehicles on the streets and the F-16s flying by above the bay.

The locals walk up the three hundred-odd steps to meditate at the feet of a great gold Buddha in the highest temple. They light candles and incense, and drape strings of flowers over the dais as offerings, and pray, and mostly ignore us tourists, who are there for less noble reasons.

There is depth here, but I can't find the doorway into it. It's time to go south, to other beaches, and hope a story will find me there.

Item: The Travel Writer has a column due, thank God.

The story finds me two weeks later, on another beach. It finds me because I've got a deadline for my monthly column in Ketchum's *Idaho Mountain Express* newspaper. It finds me because I know my audience, mostly retired folks whose religion is the Free Market and whose idea of a party is Republican. I usually write my column in the First-Person-Piss-You-Off, which you won't find in a grammar book, but it exists. It's going to be easier than usual this time because I'm on a tropical island sitting on the edge of a pool with a beer and a plate of Pad Thai and Sun Valley is freezing and snowless and dark and depressed.

It's a story I couldn't have written if I hadn't spent the time in Prachuap Kiri Khan. That earlier failure isn't wasted.

Here it is, titled:

If You Build It, They Might Not Come

We are at Nai Yang Beach, a sheltered stretch of sand on the northwest coast of Thailand's Phuket Island. It's a tourist area, and December is high season, but thus far we've seen more hotel workers, taxi drivers, bartenders, and bar girls than fellow tourists.

Such a high ratio of help to paying guests is only normal at
Amanpuri, a high-end resort five miles down the coast, where
even the cheap rooms go for a thousand dollars a night. There,
four people attend to each guest, and bar girls aren't even allowed.
Our Thailand guidebook says Amanpuri is as close as most of us
can get to being treated like royalty, and based on my one stay
there twenty years ago, I'd have to agree.

But our hotel, the Nai Yang Beach Resort, is considerably
cheaper than Amanpuri, even cheaper than most Boise hotels. It
has three sparkling and nicely chilled pools, one with a bar, and
that's the one we've been frequenting when we're not out on the
beach. Happy hour runs from three to five P.M., which works out
to one to three A.M. Ketchum time, if you're counting. The place
is mostly empty, the people are friendly, and the food is beyond
good.

While the room we're in isn't as nice as any at Amanpuri, it
isn't 950 dollars less nice. If we don't feel royal, we at least feel
noble. But yesterday, hoping to catch a glimpse of royalty, or at
least a Russian oligarch or two, we took a walk on the beach, going
toward a vast luxury hotel occupying the headland that marks the
south end of Nai Yang Beach. It looked like a great collection of
huge Thai temples down there, and we walked to within a half-
mile of it before we realized it wasn't finished. We walked a bit
more and realized it wasn't going to be. It was a ruin.

The marble-faced rooms, all three or four hundred of them,
were windowless. Here and there trees had taken root in the walls
and terraces. The tiled swimming pool was half-filled with brack-
ish water, and the reflecting ponds between the reception area and
the beach were dry and scattered with leaves and plastic trash.

We walked past signs in Thai that may or may not have said Keep Out, and looked into dim hallways lined with dark doorways. The elevator shaft went down and down to far below ground level, and things dropped into it went splash. Stacks of marble slabs occupied the unfinished kitchen of a restaurant whose empty windows looked out on a small collection of stranded fishing boats lashed to each other during low tide. Low and level tidal flats stretched out and away to our section of the beach, where the lights of restaurants had begun to glow against the sunset.

It gets dark quickly in the tropics, and the place was feeling as if maybe Jack Nicholson was caretaking there while he finished his novel, so we walked back to our hotel.

One of the beachfront restaurants advertises Broken English Spoken Perfect, and I asked the owner about the abandoned hotel. He said it had been closed for two years, after its owners had gone bankrupt. They had been bad people, he said, and they left owing the locals a lot of money. He looked out over the empty tables of his restaurant and said that things had been bad for a while. Political conflict in Thailand, the Boxing Day tsunami, SARS, and now the economic crisis had hurt the tourist industry. There were lots of empty hotels and restaurants all over Thailand. Lots of unfinished buildings. Lots of bankruptcies. Lots of workers not going to get their money.

I was translating his broken English pretty freely, but this morning's *Bangkok Post* says that the Tourism Authority of Thailand forecasts 14.3 million tourists this year, while the Association of Hotels forecasts only 12 million, a figure sixteen percent lower. In that sixteen percent is the difference—for hundreds of thousands of people—between a viable business and no business at all.

It made me think that government statistics are optimistic lies no matter where you are. It also explained why we were paying half-price for our hotel, and why every restaurant we walked by had a person posted on the sidewalk beckoning us in, and why, in the hotel's dining room tonight, we were alone, eating in front of a couple of cooks and three wait-staff and a long table piled high with fresh-caught seafood. It explains why each sad and single middle-aged male tourist in the bars is surrounded by three or four laughing bar girls, and it explains how quickly and easily a tourist industry can get overbuilt and how vulnerable the whole endeavor can be to the slightest downturn.

It made me glad I wasn't alone and lonely and susceptible to the desperate pheromones riding the sea breeze. It made me wonder how they were doing down at Amanpuri. Probably pretty well, as the world's royalty doesn't seem to have suffered much during this recession. But I won't be able to find out. I'm no longer writing for *Travel & Leisure*, and even if the *Mountain Express* would spring for it, in a world of bankruptcies and unpaid workers, I've lost the innocent ability to enjoy myself at a thousand dollars a night.

Item: Sergeant Friday's list of travel facts that will never make it onto the pages of Travel & Leisure.

- The amount of energy that it takes to fly a 747 full of tourists from Los Angeles to the Great Pyramid of Cheops is equal to the amount of energy it took to build the Great Pyramid of Cheops.

- A one-meter rise in world sea level will drown Bangladesh, the Maldives, Kiribati, and the resort beaches of the world. Beachfront hotels will topple into the surf. A two-meter rise will require the relocation of most coastal cities. If the Greenland ice cap melts, the world's oceans will rise eight meters.

- Greenland is losing eighty cubic miles of ice every year. Above the Bay of Bengal, you can fly over water that once was half-acre farms.

- Coral reefs are dying all over the world. Snorkelers look down through cloudy water at vast mud-covered skeletal cities, empty of life.

- Tourism is not just physically polluting. It's spiritually polluting as well. It's a Potemkin experience.

- Eco-tourism is a contradiction of terms. Sex tourism is a contradiction of terms. Historical tourism is a contradiction of terms.

- Industrial civilization is about to run into the Second Law of Thermodynamics. The world is running out of oil.

- Industrial civilization is about to run into Chaos Theory as the climate makes bigger and quicker moves than cause and effect would suggest. You can never see all the causes. You can never see all the effects.

- Industrial civilization is switching to slavery as an energy source. By most definitions of involuntary servitude, there are more slaves now than at any time in history.

- Civilizations and the people in them die when they exceed

their resource base. Absent fossil fuels, the sustainable-over-
time population of the planet is a billion people or less.

Sergeant Friday looks at the list and decides to become a
police detective in Los Angeles, where the facts aren't quite as
disturbing.

**_Item: The real story was there all the time and the Travel Writer
couldn't see it._**

Our last day in Prachuap Kiri Khan was Thailand's Father's Day,
the birthday of the king. Father's Day is always the birthday of
the king. New king, new Father's Day.

But for now it was December 5, and that's when I went down
to the lobby to check the weather at home. While I was there I
overheard voices coming in slow, carefully recited English from
the kitchen.

"Thank you for being our new father. Thank you for sending
us to school. Thank you for our jobs."

There is awkward laughter, and a German-accented reply:
"Thank you for being my family."

Then they all came out of the kitchen. It was the woman I
thought owned the Sun Beach Resort, and her three children,
and the German guy who'd been hanging around the lobby.

Three weeks later, floating down the Mekong River in a
slow boat, hoping that the jungle on either bank would bring
me a _Travel & Leisure_ story, I began to ask some questions about
our time at the Sun Beach: Does the Thai woman really own
it? Or is the dirtbag German the alcoholic scion of a wealthy

sportswear manufacturer, sent off to Thailand with a monthly remittance? Did he take that remittance and buy a half-share in a hotel so he could sit and drink in a place where they couldn't kick him out? Or is he the official manager for a European consortium that built the hotel, and did he hire an aging local bar girl as assistant manager, and has she brought her children in as hired help, and have they been doing such a good job he has nothing to do? Has this family adopted the German, taken him into their family as a father, and given him the first real family he's ever had? Is Thailand a conservative culture where people need a father, real or imagined, for their own identity and agency? Or are they just milking this guy for his unemployment money, just like the last ten Europeans that sat in the lobby and drank rice whiskey? Is all this fatherhood stuff just smoke up his schnitzel?

My first impulse is to answer these questions with fiction, but while that fiction would allow the interrogation of a few discrete selves, nonfiction would be an interrogation of the world and an assessment of its collective guilt. Collective guilt is something I've become interested in as a tourist and as an American.

So I should have asked the guy for his story. Expatriates everywhere like to talk, and they say things to strangers they would never say at home. I could have gotten the story of Prachuap Kiri Khan through the story of a man who's been there a while, who speaks English well enough to spill secrets, and who has maybe penetrated as far into the culture as it's possible for a Westerner to penetrate. That was the story—a profile instead of a confession—and I missed it.

There's only one thing to do: go back next November to the

Sun Beach, buy a pint of Mekong, and be sitting with it at a table in the lobby when the guy comes down for breakfast. The intern at the *Travel & Leisure* editorial offices is going to really like this idea.

One Final Rule for Writers

It's a beautiful day, filled with infinite possibility. Get your butt in that chair.

Bibliography

Many of these books are available in multiple editions. I have listed either the edition I consulted for this book or the original edition (if it is still available).

Abbott, Jack Henry. *In the Belly of the Beast: Letters from Prison.* New York: Random House, 1981.

———. *My Return.* Amherst: Prometheus, 1987.

Alther, Lisa. *Other Women.* New York: Knopf, 1984.

Andersen, Hans Christian. "The Little Match Girl" in *Hans Christian Andersen: The Complete Fairy Tales and Stories (Anchor Folktale Library).* Translated by Erik Christian Haugaard. New York: Doubleday, 1973.

Ardinger, Richard, ed. Interview of Ezra Pound by Allen Ginsberg in *What Thou Lovest Well Remains: 100 Years of Ezra Pound.* Boise: Limberlost, 1986.

Atwood, Margaret. *Bluebeard's Egg and Other Stories.* New York: Vintage, 1998.

Bakhtin, Mikhail. *Problems of Dostoevsky's Poetics.* Edited and translated by Caryl Emerson. Minneapolis: University of Minnesota Press, 1984.

Barthes, Roland. *Camera Lucida.* Translated by Richard Howard. New York: Hill and Wang, 2000.

Becker, Ernest. *The Denial of Death.* New York: Free Press Paperbacks, 1997.

Blake, William. "To Nobodaddy" in *The Complete Poetry and Prose of William Blake (Newly Revised Edition).* Edited by David V. Erdman. New York: Anchor, 1988.

Bly, Robert. "A Home in Dark Grass" in *Selected Poems.* New York: HarperCollins, 1991.

Boccaccio, Giovanni. *The Decameron.* Translated by Mark Musa and Peter Bondanella. New York: Signet Classics, 2002.

Borges, Jorge Luis. "The Garden of the Forking Paths" in *Labyrinths: Selected Stories and Other Writings.* Edited by Donald A. Yates and James E. Irby. New York: New Directions, 1964.

Campbell, Joseph. *The Hero with a Thousand Faces.* Novato, Calif.: New World Library, 2008.

Camus, Albert. *The Myth of Sisyphus and Other Essays.* Translated by Justin O'Brien. New York: Vintage, 1955.

———. *The Rebel: An Essay on Man in Revolt.* Translated by Anthony Bower. New York: Vintage, 1956.

Carver, Raymond. "A Small Good Thing" in *Where I'm Calling From: New and Selected Stories.* New York: Vintage, 1989.

———. "What We Talk About When We Talk About Love" in *Where I'm Calling From: New and Selected Stories.* New York: Vintage, 1989.

Cheever, John. "Goodbye, My Brother" in *The Stories of John Cheever.* New York: Vintage, 1978.

Conrad, Joseph. *Heart of Darkness.* London: Penguin, 1985.

Conrad, Joseph. *The Secret Sharer and Other Stories*. Mineola, New York: Dover, 1993.

Creeley, Robert. "A Wicker Basket" in *The Collected Poems of Robert Creeley, 1945-1975*. Berkeley: University of California Press, 2006.

Didion, Joan. *Slouching Toward Bethlehem*. New York: Simon and Schuster, 1979.

Dostoevsky, Fyodor. *The Possessed*. Barnes & Noble Classics, 2004.

Eliot, T.S. *The Waste Land and Other Poems*. New York: Harvest, 1962.

Ellison, Ralph. *Invisible Man*. New York: Vintage, 1952.

Ellroy, James. *The Black Dahlia*. New York: Mysterious Press, 1998.

Faulkner, William. *Absalom, Absalom!* New York: Vintage, 1972.

———. Nobel Prize Acceptance Speech, December 10, 1950. Copyright © The Nobel Foundation.

———. *The Sound and the Fury*. New York: Vintage, 1946.

Fisher, Vardis. *Orphans in Gethsemane: A Novel of the Past in the Present*. Denver: Alan Swallow, 1960.

Gelber, Jack. *The Connection*. New York: Grove, 1969.

Golding, William. *Free Fall*. New York: Harbinger, 1962.

Gramsci, Antonio. *Selections from the Prison Notebooks*. International Publishers, 1971.

Hemingway, Ernest. "Big Two-Hearted River" in *The Short Stories of Ernest Hemingway*. New York: Charles Scribner's Sons, 1966.

———. Nobel Prize Acceptance Speech, December 10, 1954. Copyright © The Nobel Foundation.

———. *The Old Man and the Sea*. New York: Charles Scribner's Sons, 1955.

Hemingway, Ernest. *The Sun Also Rises*. New York: Charles Scribner's Sons, 1954.

Hillman, James. *Dream and the Underworld*. New York: Harper and Row, 1979.

———. "Extending the Family" in *A Blue Fire*. New York: HarperPerennial, 1991.

———. *Suicide and the Soul*. Putnam, Connecticut: Spring Publications, 1997.

Hobbes, Thomas. *Leviathan*. Seven Treasures, 2009.

Hoeg, Peter. *Borderliners*. Translated by Barbara Haveland. New York: Farrar, Straus and Giroux, 1994.

Jackson, Shirley. *The Lottery and Other Stories*. New York: Farrar, Straus, 1949.

Joy, Bill. "Why the Future Doesn't Need Us." *Wired Magazine*, April 2000.

Jung, Carl. "Answer to Job" in *The Portable Jung*. Edited by Joseph Campbell. New York: Penguin, 1984.

———. *The Spirit of Man in Art and Literature*. New York: Routledge, 1984.

Kaczynski, Ted. *Unabomber Manifesto*. http://cyber.eserver.org/unabom.txt.

Kaplan, Louise J. *Female Perversions*. Northvale, New Jersey: Jason Aronson, 1997.

Laing, R.D. *The Politics of Experience*. New York: Ballantine, 1968.

———. *The Politics of the Family and Other Essays*. New York: Pantheon, 1971.

LeCarre, John. *The Tailor of Panama*. New York: Vintage, 1996.

Mailer, Norman. *The Castle in the Forest*. New York: Random House, 2007.

Marcus Aurelius. *Meditations*. Translated by Maxwell Staniforth. New York: Penguin, 2005.

McCarthy, Cormac. *The Road*. New York: Vintage, 2006.

Melville, Herman. "Bartelby the Scrivener." *Billy Budd, Sailor and Other Tales*. New York: Oxford University Press, USA, 2009.

————. "Billy Budd, Sailor." *Billy Budd, Sailor and Other Tales*. New York: Oxford University Press, USA, 2009.

————. *Moby Dick: Or The White Whale*. New York: Signet Classic, 1961.

Mitchell, Stephen, trans. *The Book of Job*. New York: HarperPerennial, 1992.

————. *Gilgamesh*. New York: Free Press, 2006.

Nietzsche, Friedrich. *Thus Spoke Zarathustra*. Translated by Walter Kaufmann. New York: Viking, 1966.

Oates, Joyce Carol. *Where Are You Going, Where Have You Been? Selected Early Stories*. Princeton: Ontario Review Books, 1994.

O'Connor, Flannery. *A Good Man is Hard to Find and Other Stories*. San Diego: Harcourt Brace, 1977.

O'Neill, Eugene. *Long Day's Journey Into Night*. New Haven: Yale University Press, 1976.

————. *Three Plays: Desire Under The Elms, Strange Interlude, Mourning Becomes Electra*. New York: Vintage, 1995.

Pinter, Harold. *The Homecoming*. New York: Grove, 1994.

Pound, Ezra. *The Cantos of Ezra Pound*. New York: New Directions, 1996.

Pynchon, Thomas. *The Crying of Lot 49*. New York: Bantam, 1966.

Pynchon, Thomas. *Gravity's Rainbow*. New York: Bantam, 1973.

———. *V.* New York: Bantam, 1973.

Romero, George A. *Dawn of the Dead*. 1978.

Russell, Bertrand. "On History" in *Philosophical Essays*. New York: Routledge, 1994.

Shaw, George Bernard. *Man and Superman*. Baltimore: Penguin, 1962.

Sontag, Susan. *On Photography*. New York: Picador, 1977.

Sophocles. *Oedipus The King*. Translated by Bernard M. W. Knox. New York: Pocket Books, 1972.

Stegner, Wallace. *The Sound of Mountain Water: The Changing American West*. New York: E. P. Hutton, 1980.

Steinbeck, John. Nobel Prize Acceptance Speech, December 10, 1962. Copyright © The Nobel Foundation.

Tannen, Deborah. "Marked Women, Unmarked Men." *The New York Times Magazine*, June 20, 1993.

Veblen, Thorstein. *The Theory of the Leisure Class*. New York: Oxford University Press, USA, 2008.

Vonnegut, Kurt. "Knowing What's Nice." September 24, 2003. The Web Vonnegut Archives. http://www.vonnegutweb.com/archives/arc_nice.html.

Warren, Robert Penn. *All the King's Men*. New York: Bantam, 1963.

Whitman, Walt. "Leaves of Grass." *The Complete Poems of Walt Whitman*. London: Wordsworth Editions, 1998.

Williams, Tennessee. *The Theater of Tennessee Williams, Vol. 3: Cat on a Hot Tin Roof / Orpheus Descending / Suddenly Last Summer*. New York: New Directions, 1991.

Zipes, Jack, trans. "Hansel and Gretel" in *The Complete Fairy Tales of the Brothers Grimm*. New York: Bantam, 2003.

Permissions Acknowledgments

Index

John Rember is a fourth-generation Idahoan. Recurring themes in his writing include the meaning of place, the impact of tourism on the West, and the weirdness of everyday life.

His books include the memoir *Traplines: Coming Home to Sawtooth Valley* (Vintage: 2004), and two collections of short stories, *Cheerleaders from Gomorrah: Tales from the Lycra Archipelago* (Confluence: 1994) and *Coyote in the Mountains* (Limberlost: 1989). He has also published numerous articles and columns in magazines and newspapers, including *Travel & Leisure, Wildlife Conservation,* and *The Huffington Post.* He has been a professor of writing for many years, most recently as a core faculty member of the Pacific University MFA program (Forest Grove, Oregon). He is Writer at Large at The College of Idaho.

LaVergne, TN USA
26 January 2011
213994LV00004B/126/P